The ten-year-old John Lane was, in 1933, one of a party of fifty child emigrants bound from England for a new life at Kingsley Fairbridge Farm School in Western Australia.

At the age of two John Lane had been placed into the care of Dr Barnardo's Homes near London, and soon after went to a foster family in the idyllic rural Cotswolds for six years – the happiest years of his life. But in 1932 he was plucked, without any reason given, from the only love and security he had ever experienced and returned to the shattering experiences of institutional care.

Fairbridge Kid, describes in authentic detail how a barefoot army of three hundred children were transported halfway around the world to be trained and disciplined in a semi-military environment preparatory to being sent out, at the age of sixteen, to work as farm labourers and domestics.

John Lane provides a moving account of how, despite the best intentions and personal sacrifice of many genuine people to help the underprivileged, there is, for children like 'the Fairbridge Kids', no substitute for the warm love of parents and family.

Cover painting by Jillian Green.

John Lane was born in England in 1922 and in 1924 was placed into an orphanage, being registered, with his mother's surname, as Jack Kenneth Ramsbottom. In 1933 he was sent to Kingsley Fairbridge Farm School in Western Australia. He joined the Australian Army during World War Two, was captured at the fall of Singapore, and was a P.O.W. for three and a half years, mostly in Japan.

After the war, he decided to discard his association with Jack Ramsbottom and resume his life with the legally acquired name of John Lane. After a career with the Australian Army Music Corps, culminating with teaching music at the Army School of Music in Victoria, he has now retired.

John Lane's first book, *Summer Will Come Again*, was published in 1987 and is an account of his experiences as a P.O.W. in Japan.

John Lane

FAIRBRIDGE KID

FAIRBRIDGE KID

JOHN LANE

FREMANTLE ARTS CENTRE PRESS

First published 1990 by
FREMANTLE ARTS CENTRE PRESS
193 South Terrace (PO Box 320), South Fremantle
Western Australia 6162.

Reprinted 1990, 1995, 1997.

Consultant Editor Helen Bradbury.
Designed by John Douglass.
Production Coordinator Linda Martin.

Typeset by Fremantle Arts Centre Press
and printed by Lamb Print.

National Library of Australia
Cataloguing-in-publication data

Lane, John, 1922 -.
Fairbridge Kid.

ISBN 1 86368 000 4

I. Lane, John, 1922 –. 2. Orphans – Western Australia
– Biography. 3. Orphans – Great Britain – Biography. 4.
Orphanages – Western Australia. 5. Orphanages –
Great Britain. I. Title.

362.7'3'0924

To Ronda
It took so long to find you.

ACKNOWLEDGEMENTS

I wish to thank Collette Bradford and Lyn Clargo of Barnardo's Barkingside Headquarters in Ilford, Essex, for giving me copies of records and photographs from my personal file. My thanks also to Mrs Ethel Toussaint for her historical photographs of Mandurah, and to Patricia Hanson for her gift of photographs from the album of her late Aunt Rose (a former Fairbridge Farm cottage mother).

A special thank you to Mrs Daphne Powell for lending me her collection of 'The Fairbridgian' magazines from which much valuable material was gained. Acknowledgement is also due to the J.S. Battye Library of West Australian History for the photograph on page 86.

For locating my foster parent's grave and giving me the only photograph I have of Mrs Nobes, I am forever grateful to Arthur Johnson.

John Lane

The creative writing programme of Fremantle Arts Centre Press is assisted by the Australia Council, the Australian Federal Government's arts funding and advisory body.

Fremantle Arts Centre Press receives financial support from the Western Australian Department for the Arts.

CONTENTS

Preface   11

Blissful Ignorance   13
'Ramsarse' the Wretched   21
Pennies from Heaven   29
Life's Unpredictable Cycle   40
Clapham   52
A Change of Fortune   67
South Bound   76
Dinkum Aussies in the Making   85
Fairbridge: the Village and the Man   102
Standard Four Urchin   122
An Aussie Holiday   138
New Chums No More   157
Unpalatable Rice and Fresh Apricots   171
Fairbridge Seniors   186
Working the Farm   203
Sailing Before the Wind   212
Revelations   223

Epilogue   237

Full lasting is the song, though he,
The singer, passes; lasting too,
For souls not lent in usury,
The rapture of the forward view.

With that I bear my senses fraught
Till what I am fast shoreward drives.
They are the vessel of the thought,
The vessel splits, the thought survives.

Kingsley Fairbridge.

PREFACE

In trying to recall so many distant events there is a distinct possibility that I may have inadvertently accredited the occasional character with an uncommitted incident. If so, please accept my apology. Wherever possible, I have used correct names. Only in isolated cases, and to avoid embarrassment, has a name been scrambled.

It would have been far easier for me to have remained an anonymous relic of a distant empire-building scheme, only vaguely remembered by ageing Old Fairbridgians. However, as a first hand record of this remarkable era seemed unlikely to be forthcoming, I decided to re-open old wounds in order to reveal an accurate story of its time.

John Lane

Jack Ramsbottom (John Lane), aged fourteen months, 1924.

BLISSFUL IGNORANCE

I was almost sixteen years of age before I discovered who I was. Until that incredible moment of truth, I just assumed that I had been born in England in November 1922. My parents had not told me that. I had never heard of my parents. Somewhere along the way, being shunted in and out of children's institutions, I had acquired the information. It probably came from a foster family with whom I had spent seven idyllic years in the English countryside. Now, on the threshold of manhood, I found myself 25,000 kilometres away across the world near the capital city of Perth in Western Australia in yet another institution called Fairbridge Farm School.

Never on any occasion was I consulted nor asked whether any of these multiple changes in my life was desirable to me. Never was I given the choice. For almost sixteen years my life was directed by an unseen force. Like a marionette dangling at the end of a string, I had been held in an all-embracing grip, powerless to withstand the manipulative whim of the master controller. I had been conditioned well. On any given command I performed instantly and obediently. My subjugation had been complete.

Why then, did I have to wait almost sixteen years for this flush of release? What were the circumstances that led to the loosening of ties and a severance of the controlling strings that had sent me crashing to the ground in a tumbled heap? Struggling to my feet, I had made the miraculous discovery that the shackles of the past no longer bound me. Now, physically, I was free. The mental cleansing took a moment longer. A few deep breaths of unpolluted Western Australian air went straight to my head and ousted all residual doubts and restrictions. Stimulated by an unfamiliar oxygenation, my undeveloped brain cells burst immediately into life begging for recognition. So much of my past remained a mystery. A barrage of questions now fairly clamoured for answers.

Why had I been placed in the care of Dr Barnardo's Homes? Why, after spending so many years in the love and security of a foster family, had I been so suddenly taken away and thrust back into a crowded orphanage? Why had I been packed aboard a ship to be sent from one institution in England to another institution in far-off Australia? Did I have any real parents, and if so, where were they? And above all, how did I manage to finish up with the name of Jack Ramsbottom?

The answers to these questions originate with the circumstances of my birth and the subsequent first four years of my life, about which I have no recollection. Later revelations proved this void to be fortuitous to the point of being merciful. My reminiscential life, in fact, started blissfully enough under the care and love showered upon me by a compassionate substitute family.

Tucked away in the seclusion of the Cotswold Hills, almost forgotten by time, Sam and Rosa Nobes lived in one of a handful of stone cottages that formed the hamlet of Bismore in the county of Gloucestershire, England. The whitish-grey scattering of cottages clung to the lower slopes of a hill below the more populous village of Eastcombe that tumbled over the crest of the Cotswold plateau. Across the way stretched the wooded hills cradling the enchanting beauty of Toadsmoor Valley. A narrow stream crept cautiously from far off trees like a fawn grazing leisurely through a meadow, before disappearing beneath the track that twisted its way to Stroud. In the opposite direction, skirting a small copse of beech trees, the narrow dirt track climbed its way up

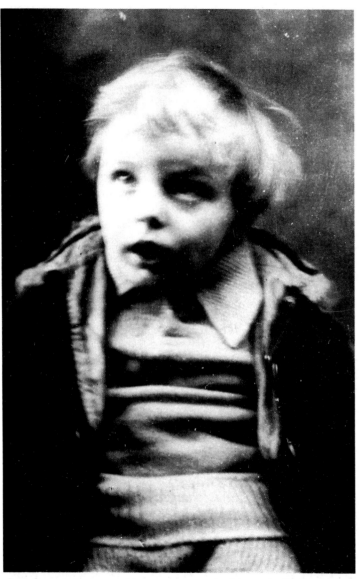

Jack Ramsbottom, aged two years, on admittance to Dr. Barnado's, 11.11.1925.

The hamlet of Bismore, on the outskirts of Eastcombe. The Nobe's cottage is in the middle distance, just above and to the right of the centre of the photograph.

into Eastcombe. In the 1930s Eastcombe was a village of children.

It was into this spacious environment of pure bracing air that Dr Barnardo, as far back as 1880 decided to board out some of his host of orphans, free from the contamination of the cities. Eastcombe suited his requirements perfectly: Its strong Baptist community ensured a supply of the Christian foster-parents on which the Society insisted.

Records show that I was just two years old when I was placed into Dr Barnardo's Village Home in the London suburb of Barkingside. Ten months later I was fostered out to the Nobes family.

As I grew up, Mr and Mrs Nobes quite naturally became my father and mother, and Mother's sister was Auntie Flo. During my seven-year stay with them I shared one of three upstairs bedrooms with my foster-brothers who seemed to come and go at irregular intervals. That is, all except George Brown. George and I survived the longest, and as a result, we grew as close as any pair of natural brothers.

The ground floor of our cottage consisted of a large kitchen/dining room, a living room, a scullery and a pantry. There was no bathroom, no running water, no electricity. Water was collected in barrels grouped outside the back door and connected to the guttering by a movable downpipe. Paraffin lamps and candles supplied the lighting. The lavatory was twenty paces down the back garden path. A neatly cut bundle of newspaper squares threaded on a string hung from a nail on the wall, and on a small makeshift shelf rested a stub of a candle in an enamel holder and a box of safety matches. Once a week Father changed the pan. Further down the back garden was an open-sided shed and the woodheap.

In the front, Father had worked the half-hectare of sloping ground into a vegetable garden. He had to. Times were tough and there was little work about. Mother said how lucky we were to have so much land when most of the other villagers had only small plots of ground at the Eastcombe allotment gardens up on the fringe of the plain.

Father was a big-framed fresh-faced man with thinning sandy-coloured hair that could have been auburn in his youth. Then he was nearly fifty and there was a strangeness about him that frightened me. His severe speech impediment prevented us from communicating, a situation which quite often left him terribly frustrated. When I was old enough to understand, Mother explained that he had survived both the Boer War and World War I — but at a cruel cost.

'It be the madness of men that caused so much suffering', she went on with a rare bitterness in her voice. 'Thousands of young'uns in the Great War died horrible choking deaths when they were shelled with poisonous gasses. Father was one of the lucky ones — and you can see what it did to him.'

Mother was all giving. Childless herself, she not only displayed incredible tolerance in dealing with Father's affliction, but had devoted many years of her life to raising orphans. The supreme altruist, she was worshipped by a succession of foster-children to whom she gave all her love in equal portions. Many of her 'children' after reaching adulthood, still returned to see her. Florence and John Bottomley paid regular visits, and never failed to take me on a special outing. Life was wonderful.

With brother George at school, my activities were restricted to the house and garden, which was still a sizeable play ground. My pre-school activities included racing imaginary motor vehicles around the paths. George taught me all I knew about cars and bikes. Our hills were among the toughest in the Cotswolds, a feature which guaranteed frequent trail events. Whenever the 'machines' tackled the obstacles we had placed on the sharp bends and turns, he'd point out the B.S.A.s, the Nortons, the Ariels, and half a dozen other makes. But the pick of them all was my Rudge Whitworth motorcycle. To me, Rudge had the sound of power. It was the noise I made when revving the engine. It not only rolled easily off the tongue, but after a little experimenting, I found that when used in combination with a growl, it sounded just like the real thing. Rrudge-rrudge-rrudge and away I'd race, scorching past the gooseberry bushes, screeching around corners; even coming to grief occasionally. Whether this early brief period of contrived misfortune created a regular, repetitive pattern throughout my life, I shall never know, but it seems that from then on, scarcely a day has passed when I haven't sustained a cut, or bruise, or sprain, or something worse. Suffice it to say that my days of feigning injury began and finished with those unique races on that 'murderous' circuit.

But my pre-school days weren't all filled with play. I remember helping my father to dig potatoes. As he forked them out of the soil, I filled my special pint-sized bucket and carted them off to the shed for bagging. The trip took me along the lower path that ran the length of a sharp two-metre drop into a gully that must have been the most fertile strip of land we had. Along its entire length grew a prolific crop of head-high stinging nettles, so rich in yield, that had a trophy been awarded for the best display, Father would have won in perpetuity. At best, the stinging nettles protected our lower boundary from sneak attacks by tramps and gypsies, while at worst, a fall over the embankment would be only marginally less disastrous than a trip to hell, which even at the age of four, I knew was a most undesirable destination. At any rate, with a potential disaster area so close, it was a powerful stimulus for concentration.

Apart from the garden, there was little else I could do to help. When I did try to lighten Father's workload in the harvesting of the currant and gooseberry crops, my efforts went unappreciated. There was no small amount of conjecture amongst the family as to the phenomenon of a failed yield. What had promised to have been a bumper season one year had strangely been affected by a mysterious loss of fruit just prior to its ripening. No adverse weather conditions had been experienced, no unusual insect activity had been observed, and no marauding flock of birds had invaded our territory. Apparently none of the family had counted on the guile and cunning, not to mention the appetite of one small child. I still pride myself on the skill of my operation, and, even now, think that my exploits would have remained undiscovered if I had not been untimely and suddenly stricken with acute diarrhoea, an illness that, under the circumstances would have earned me little sympathy, but for the severity of the attack. As it was, further punishment was unnecessary. The drastic consequence of my action was enough to effect a promise from me to undertake no more raids on family fruit bushes.

So far as I can remember, there were only two more attacks on my life at that time; one by my brother George, and one unintentional 'suicide' attempt. The self-inflicted injury happened when I was cleaning a jagged piece of jam-jar over one of the water-butts and nearly severed my fingers off one hand.

The other near miss for me came from being too trustful of my brother. Sunday morning was the only chance the family had of sleeping in, but for us boys it meant little other than finding something to do for the extra hour before breakfast. George as usual came to the rescue with a new game — bum fights. Dressed only in our long night-shirts, the idea was to position ourselves back-to-back on the bed-top and trade bump for bump with our backsides. Predictably, the game got out of control, and in the end I don't know who or what made the most noise; my bellow of anguish as I flew across the bedroom, the crack of my skull hitting a thick porcelain object, or Mother's cry of despair and look of horror as she burst into the room. But despite Mother's distress, it was nothing in comparison to my impending fate. It wasn't so much the fear of being hurt that troubled me, as the terrifying prospect of landing in our well-placed jerry. George's earlier positioning had been uncannily accurate. The one redeeming feature in my favour, and perhaps a life-saving detail, was the fact that the jerry was only half full.

'RAMSARSE' THE WRETCHED

Having survived enough of life's perils in my pre-school years to have lasted a normal boy a complete childhood, my first day at school just before my fifth birthday presented a hazard of bizarre proportions.

Up to that day I was not unduly made aware of my uncommon surname. What I did know was that I was a Barnardo child, that the Nobeses were not my real parents, that Mother's sister was Aunt Flo, my brother was George, and that I was Jack. So far as I was concerned, although I knew my surname wasn't Nobes, there hadn't been any occasion to warrant any bother about what it actually was. But after Mother had walked me up the Bismore hill to present me to the principal of the Baptist school, it all changed. Whatever preliminaries were required Mother was taking care of it; I was far too excited to worry about mundane matters such as registration. After pestering George for months to take me with him up to school, all the disappointments and frustrations of the past were forgotten now that the day had actually arrived. At last I was one of the 'big kids'.

Mother hovered in the background until I was seated, then departed the scene obviously relieved in the knowledge that I had settled in quite happily. That agreeable state of affairs lasted the entire morning, interrupted only by the pleasant recess period in which a hot cup of Horlicks was

Eastcombe Baptist School.

provided, which helped considerably to augment the school's piped heating system.

With lunch came the first fraternising with the children from the other classes, an association that brought pleasantries to a halt and confrontation to the fore. A belligerent looking redhead was the first to make an approach.

'My name's Eddie Collins, what's yours?'

'I'm Jack Ramsbottom.'

'Ramsbottom? What a funny name! Fancy having a name like Ramsbottom!' With that, he galloped away shouting his head off that the new kid's name was Ramsbottom ha, ha, ha.

I just stood still not knowing what to do. I was going through my first painful experience of embarrassment. The name hadn't troubled me before; none of the family had made a joke of it. The fact was that I'd only remembered being called Jack. I'd scarcely given my surname a thought; the sound of it surprised me, it caught me off guard. After a few minutes' thought I had to admit it was a strange name; ridiculous almost. The same label on anyone else would have been hilarious. But the unhappy fact was that somehow or other, whether I liked it or not, I was the one who was saddled with it.

At that stage, I was far too young to work out the derivation of names, or how I had managed to procure my hapless tag. It did occur to me however, that the state of being motherless and fatherless should have been stigma enough for one person to bear, without having the added ordeal of being subjected to ridicule about a name, a circumstance over which I had no control. I had accepted the fact that I was parentless. I was a Nobes child now. From as far back as I could remember they had kept me warm, fed, and loved. In their care I was happy and content. Now, on my first day at school that secure protective blanket of warmth and affection was being stripped from me. I felt exposed and vulnerable.

This sudden crisis in my life was a new experience; an introduction to unfamiliar and disturbing emotions. There was no escaping the deluge of taunts, the innuendos, the sniggers and the outright belly laughs that accompanied me wherever I went on the playground. I had the distinction of bearing a name that humoured other kids, yet left me confused, bewildered and hurt. I had no answer to their jibes.

However, it could have been worse. There was some consolation in the fact that most of the children at the Baptist church were Dr Barnardo kids, fostered throughout Eastcombe. That was something we had in common. There were no grounds for taunting there.

But I found that as the weeks went by, the novelty of my name gradually wore off and I became accepted as just another of the adopted village kids. Perhaps having George around was a distinct advantage. His size practically guaranteed me a civilized reception from well over half the school. From then on I mostly got Jack, Jackie or Rammy. But always on official occasions I was given the full treatment of Ramsbottom.

These official activities usually brought schooling to a halt and spread apprehension amongst the children. If the conversion of the classroom was to a temporary hospital, there was less concern. Mothers knew their offspring were either being swabbed for throat infections or being deloused. Children thought they were either being strangled or scalped.

It was when a classroom took on the appearance of a dental surgery that terror swept through the school. Those who knew what was coming trembled visibly at the thought; newcomers, like myself, froze in fright at the ordeal awaiting us.

It was on one such occasion while trapped in the clutches of the dental chair that, incidentally, I discovered to what extent a professional person is prepared to perjure himself in the name of humanity. 'This might hurt a bit', the man said unsympathetically, pedalling away on the ancient contraption. With my mouth full of thumb and fingers, I was in no position to argue or even to comment. Somehow or other he found enough room to insert the nasty end of the drill and from then on I wished I hadn't been born.

Whether it was my muffled cry, the kick on the shins, or merely the bitten finger of the dentist that did the trick, I shall never know. All I did feel at that moment was the relief of spitting blood, bone, and water into a funnel that a nurse obligingly held for me. Then after a reassuring smile, she coaxed me back into the sacrificial couch where I was plugged and scraped until it was decided that I'd had enough treatment for one sitting.

I suppose it could be said that the greatest inconvenience about a visit to the dentist these days, is the loss of feeling to the mouth while the effects of the local anaesthesia wears off. During my childhood at Eastcombe there was no such problem. We simply went without that refinement.

Later in the afternoon when school came out for the day, Eddie Collins lay in wait for me. Bullying was not his only attribute. High on the list of his other venomous skills was his natural cunning. When my brother George was around, he left me well alone. But this afternoon, George was nowhere in sight. Seizing his opportunity, the bully let me have it. 'What twer you bawling about Ramsbottom?' Pressing on the advantage of a captive audience without George, he snarled to anyone within earshot, 'Hey, did you hear Ramsarse snivelling in the dentist's chair today? Did the nasty man hurt your mouth Sheepsbum? He should've clipped your ears as well!' And on and on he went. Coming on top of the dentist's drill, the taunts hurt as much as the physical pain. I made my tearful way home confused and bewildered until I collapsed into the tranquillity of Mother's arms.

Although I was too young to be troubled by it, the Great Depression forced most families into an extremely frugal existence. Jobs were scarce and money was tight. People worked long hours to earn barely enough for the necessities of life. Luxury was a forgotten word. The closest my parents came to it was to sit down to a simple supper of bread and cheese on a Saturday night, and wash it down with the pint of beer that Father had carried home in a jug from the Lamb Inn up in Eastcombe.

Even though the Nobeses received an allowance from Barnardo's for our upkeep, I doubt if it was nearly enough to cover the cost of keeping us, particularly the way George and I went through our clothes. But we grew up to accept the conditions as being normal. Every child in the village knew that our recreation activities depended on improvisation and resourcefulness. For example the simple game of 'conkers' kept the school entertained for weeks without costing a penny, although there was often a price to pay in the form of torn britches or ripped shirts when climbing the chestnut trees in search of the raw material.

Other games came and went at fairly predictable intervals,

but perhaps it was some medieval West Country law of procedure that transformed an empty main street one day into a battlefield of flying saucers the next. Actually the 'saucers' were tops, set into motion by hand or string, and launched into orbit by the vigorous flogging from a home-made whip. Competitions were held to see who could gain the best distance, an exploit fraught with danger as missiles frequently disappeared only to crash through someone's front window. One advantage of the times was the almost non-existent likelihood of seeing your best drive of the day shatter someone's windscreen. Very few automobiles made it into Eastcombe.

Just as abruptly as it started, tops would be out and, in a few days, replaced by something else. In the meantime, with any sort of luck, the thrill of a lifetime might overtake us...

The most spectacular event to shatter the tranquillity of our part of the Cotswolds was the motor-bike trials. It was the unanticipated suddenness with which these competitions materialised that made them so exciting. No warning was given. The first inkling someone had of the unusual happening, was the sound of the trail blazer's bike coughing its way through the village while the rider scattered red powder that marked the way for the oncoming contestants. Every boy and most of the men in the village recognised that sound. The news spread faster than an outbreak of measles, and children prepared for action. If there was one activity short of war that could unite the villagers, this was it. Today, the adversaries were the motor cycle riders and the objective was to make their passage through our hills as difficult as possible.

Without a word being spoken or an order given, every lad went to action stations. In an extraordinary feat of engineering, particularly for a juvenile team of non-skilled workers, a typical Cotswold stone wall was converted into a tank trap without mechanical aid, in less than half an hour. And if the hapless riders thought they could avoid the trap by climbing around the bank, they were doomed to disappointment, if not downright disaster. The most formidable rocks had been reserved for just such an exigency, placed so compactly that an ant could scarcely have found its way through. With our landscaping finished we were surprised to find an official had joined us in admiring our efforts. At first we feared he might call in a bulldozer to dismantle our work, but his smile of approval put us at ease as he positioned himself in the most advantageous place for judging the contestants. His only concern was for the safety of some little twerp who had disappeared behind a boulder. It was decided it would be prudent to rescue him. With the obstacles in place, there was nothing to do but wait for the fun to begin.

An hour later a shout went up as someone heard the first distant gargle of an approaching bike. A moment of silence and everyone heard it. Almost immediately, another of different pitch joined in. In two minutes a noise like a swarm of angry bees was heading our way.

Now the first rider was approaching the bottom of the climb, gunning his engine to a powerful roar. Up the hill he swarmed; the revs falling away momentarily as he geared down. Closer came the moment of truth. The unsuspecting rider came relentlessly on like a soldier in battle. The tension mounted. Both my hands clutched tightly between my legs in a partially successful effort to stop a sudden urge to urinate.

When the front wheel hit the first rock, my hands went skywards in elation, while the bike shot skywards in orbit and my pants became damp. Miraculously, the rider retained control to bring his machine back to earth in a precarious but successful landing. This was an accomplishment of considerable merit in view of the bumpy nature of the ground, which from the air would have looked like fall-out from a volcanic eruption.

Time and again the young rider displayed a brilliance of technique well beyond our comprehension, but in the end the law of averages beat him. But before the end, he fought magnificently, bouncing from boulder to boulder with legs flying and motor-cycle screaming in protest, until through sheer volume of shot and shell, both bike and rider succumbed.

We kids were ecstatic. To have brought down the first contestant was a result far beyond our expectations. From the safety of the bunkers, there was no attempt to conceal our delight. Jubilant shouts of victory combined with unsympathetic cries of derision were his only reward from the juvenile gang on 'slaughter hill'. To our shame, we weren't even prepared to give the luckless man an honourable discharge, whereas the official adjudicator would have been justified in recommending him for a Victoria Cross.

But when the last competitor walked his bike through the bend, clambered onto the seat, and sped away, silence returned to the scene with a greater intensity than ever. Once again normal conversation was possible and bird calls could be heard; all that remained was the pungent smell of burnt high octane fuel. And as the spectators dispersed, and George and I made for home, I discovered that my wet pants had suddenly become cold and uncomfortable.

The performance of the motor bike trials through the village sparked a natural interest in conducting our own programme, using hoops. Every child had a hoop, which was only a discarded bicycle wheel with the spokes removed, so they cost nothing. The problem lay in finding a suitable powder for marking the course. Eventually it was decided to use old house bricks for the job. The colour was close enough; the difficulty was in finding volunteers to do the crushing. The occasion was ready-made for me to make a big name for myself; or rather I hoped the reverse would happen. Whenever an opportunity came for me to ingratiate myself with the big kids, I took it. Call it crawling or grovelling if you like, but if it meant relief from name calling, I was prepared to do it. Besides, I envied the bigger boys their status. So long as I pounded housebricks, I got fewer 'Ramsarses' and 'Sheepsarses', and more 'Little-uns', a label that was immeasurably preferable to the indignity of the former.

PENNIES FROM HEAVEN

Those villagers given to godliness were divided almost equally into two religious groups, Anglicans and Baptists, and identified as Church and Chapel goers respectively. Each denomination had its own place of worship and ran its own elementary school. Fostered Barnardo kids boosted the attendance of the Chapel, while a village Anglican orphanage ensured a continuous supply of children for the Church. From the time I started day school I had to attend Sunday School. For a year or so, weekly bribes in the shape of brightly coloured stickers and other nondescript rewards for regular attendance were enough to keep my interest in biblical history alive. But as I grew older my concentration during Sunday School time drifted increasingly to imaginary and more recent history-making adventures of my own. However, it wasn't until I turned seven that Mother allowed me to drop Sunday School. By that age, she considered that I was ready for the Sunday morning Chapel service. When the family climbed the hill together on the following Sunday, I had no idea of the surprise that awaited me.

For the first few months of Chapel, I was the envy of most of the other little kids in the congregation. George had wangled the job for me as his assistant organ-blower. The organ was built in a special loft, to which access was gained by a flight of steps just inside the main entrance. The pipes were encased in an elaborately carved frame which overlooked a double row of stained deal pews. A carved wooden balustrade featuring a central clock encompassed the organist.

The organ had to be manually pumped, a responsible job that George had been doing for some time, no doubt under Father's auspices. Watching George in action, I quickly understood the importance of the job. In order to avoid an embarrassing silence at the start of each hymn, the organ had first to be primed, so the timing was all important. The pumping had to be started just before the minister's announcement, an action that, for the uninitiated, produced an assortment of questionable noises.

But the job was not hard, so once I knew how to control the wooden handle, and mastered the timing, George let me share the work. It was some compensation for still being in the 'little-un' category, but I was not too young to realise the value of knowing the right people when favours were sought.

Both Church and Chapel celebrated certain significant religious days which, so far as us kids were concerned, were just an excuse to have a party. The Chapel crowd set the pace in a procession around the village on Whit Monday, parading banners and singing hymns, especially pausing outside the homes in which someone was sick. But the best part of the day came after Sunday School when a special tea with seed cake was put on. There were so many at this function that three sittings were required to feed them all, and with Mother wielding the teapot, it gave me the opportunity to lose myself amongst the crowd and set up chances for multiple helpings. Actually, there was an unofficial competition among the boys when we compared scores afterwards, when anyone with fewer than two was considered backward, while those with the 'possible' three, were immediately promoted to the top of the social order. I considered myself to be distinctly disadvantaged. With a name like mine, there was a tendency to remember it far more easily than the Browns and Smiths. Even so, I was satisfied with scoring twice, but with the luxury of seedcake on the menu, the scramble was on to take the maximum advantage of this rare opportunity.

The Chapel's most spectacular day came in the autumn when the Harvest Festival was celebrated. Despite the bad times, year after year, there was always a magnificent display of produce and grains to offer for blessing. Practically the whole foyer of the Chapel was a mass of colour, with tiered shelves packed with beautifully arranged sections of vegetables, fruits and flowers, home made jars of jams and pickles, and loaves of bread in all shapes and sizes.

The Anglicans, for their part, celebrated Ascension Day by holding an impressive ceremony called the Dressing of the Wells. The wells used for the occasion are a feature of the village of Bisley, about three kilometres to the north of Eastcombe. A natural spring in the village has been channelled into seven separate streams that flow through openings in a man-made concrete shrine. Around the walls is inscribed the text *Oh Ye Wells Bless Ye the Lord Praise Him and Magnify Him For Ever.*

With the adults left to make their own way to Bisley, the Church organised a special outing for the children which left from the main street outside the church, where decorated horses waited, harnessed to colourful wagons spread with seats of baled hay. Although it was a rival group's outing, no one seemed to mind the Baptist kids joining in the festivities. It was certainly something different and always a memorable day.

But for some strange reason, it nearly always rained at least part of the day. I couldn't work out, if it was such an important event in the Church's calendar, why God didn't let them have a dry day. In Sunday School, we Chapel kids had always been told to pray for the Lord's blessing; surely the Church kids would have received similar instruction. Ascension Day would have been the ideal day for the Lord's blessing, and the only reason I could think of why it rained, was that the Church people couldn't have prayed hard enough. There was no doubt about it, they usually let us down badly. Perhaps the result might have been different if both Chapel and Church kids had thought to combine their prayers in one massive plea for a fine day, but it was never done. So we got wet.

The Chapel Sunday School included in its calendar an annual train excursion to Weston-Super-Mare, which, in an era when a trip of 25 kilometres to Cheltenham was considered to be quite an adventure, by today's standards, was like going to the moon. The waiting was almost unbearable. For weeks ahead anticipation built up to such a peak that by the time the day came around, I was bursting with excitement.

As there was no direct line to Weston, we had to travel east to Swindon, then back-track on a different line. It was a roundabout way but it was all part of the outing and I enjoyed it. I liked the sound of the wheels clack-clacking and the relaxing sway of the moving carriage. I enjoyed sticking my head out of the window, relishing the clean smell of steam wafting back from the giant locomotive. There were moments of discomfort of course when specks of soot stung the exposed face or irritated the eyes. Usually these were only minor inconveniences, but if a larger piece occasionally refused to budge I had the luxury of retreating to Mother's lap to be operated upon. After her gentle treatment, I'd be quite content to recuperate in the comforting softness of her bosom while dreamily watching the cows and trees and meadows swirl by like a giant roundabout.

When we finally reached the broad Promenade and gazed out to sea, I was bewildered and confused. Where I expected the ocean to be, there was nothing but a vast expanse of mud; a dirty grey puddly mass of it stretched away until it disappeared behind a horizon of fluffy cloud.

A thin strip of sandy beach beyond the Promenade was vanishing fast beneath a growth of bathing tents, deckchairs, sprawling people and miniature castle builders. Beyond, and on the fringe of the threatening ooze, a troop of child-mounted donkeys patrolled the border between sand and slime. The contrast between home and this could not have been greater. And from out across the space swept the wind in sharp, salty gusts that whipped my face and stung my nostrils, leaving me gasping.

At one end of the beach, a giant pier straddled the potted sea bed like some prowling monster. According to George, along its length were booths of fanciful exhibits and coin-operated machines that promised a selection of mystery and horror. Without even thinking about the shops, the choice was difficult. I wanted to explore everything at once; the donkey ride, the Punch and Judy show, sand, mud, and the secrets of the pier.

For the first half hour, I saw nothing. I was too busy looking for my parents who had managed to lose me. I walked up and down the beach working myself into a panic until I was found. I think they must have recognised my whine. After that near disaster, I toddled along at my mother's heel like a scalded puppy waiting for a command while all the time hoping for a handout. And for most of the day, the marvellous woman repeatedly dived into her purse for pennies that sent George and me scampering away to spend. All the exercise in the face of the stiff breeze soon had me wishing I'd eaten my breakfast. The sandwiches Mother had packed had vanished long before, now I was compelled to bring the matter of my appetite to my parents' notice by setting up a constant chant of 'I'm hungry, I'm hungry'.

With our appetites temporarily appeased in the closest tea shop, and George and I firmly clutching a stick of candy rock, we returned to the Prom wall just in time to see the phenomenon of the incoming tide. The sea surged in so swiftly that it sent the stall holders and deck chair proprietors into frenzied activity retreating from the path of relentless water. Seeing it for the first time, I remember it as a miracle of movement, an incredible force that swept in from out of the unknown, and I wondered whether it would come sweeping on to drown us all. Having been assured by Auntie Flo that the sea wall would stop it, we headed for the pier, which by now, was looking less formidable every minute as its tall legs shrank beneath the deepening sea.

The Pier turned out to be a disappointment. With its questionable attractions given short shrift, Mother compensated by buying icecreams all round. I don't know what they cost in 1929, but whatever the price, it must have made a sizeable dent in her remaining capital. We licked as we sauntered, filling in time that once seemed destined never to arrive.

The rest of our crowd must have felt as we did because, before long, we joined a steady stream of people making for the train and the chance to rest weary feet. George was more than happy with the movement because he had been under instructions to carry me if I collapsed. With stragglers finally settled amongst the hotchpotch of nondescript packages and sprawling bodies, the long homeward ride jolted reluctantly into life. And despite the exhausted state of my little body, from somewhere deep within my sleep-racked head, there registered the fact that the moment of re-entry into our Cotswold cottage was the best part of the outing.

I must have been about seven years old before I realised that with pocket money practically non-existent, I'd have to find some paying jobs to do. Father was just not in the position to give us a weekly allowance. He never seemed to have regular work, which was not surprising in view of his difficulty in communicating. I had seen him wielding a scythe when clearing a neighbour's property, and had watched him disappear underground when digging the odd grave or two, but the combined income from these labours would hardly have paid for his weekly pint. The closest he came to having a regular job was officiating as a verger at the Chapel's two Sunday services; eleven in the morning and eight at night. For these duties he was paid out of the takings from the last evening service of each month. When he arrived home on these special nights, we kids were waiting to participate in a rite that was not to be missed at any price.

We were already seated around the large kitchen table when Father took up his position at the head. Then with an unhurried sense of timing he produced a small calico bag bulging with money. When he upended it in the centre of the table, a deluge of coins flowed across the bare boards in a magnificent display of wealth. There were a few brief moments in which to relish the spectacle, before all hands set to to sort the spoils into their relative piles. Then, in an atmosphere of tense expectation, Mother and Father counted each pile separately, which when totalled, should have amounted to exactly one pound. If it was correct, satisfaction oozed from every enquiring face. There was money in the house again. More importantly, there was something in it for us.

With deliberate ceremony, Father selected two of the shiniest pennies and handed one each to George and me. Despite the fact that the same ritual went on month after month, there was never any lessening of the suspense and drama of the occasion. But if the pound was as little as a penny short, a cloak of disappointment descended over the evening. At a time when money was so badly needed, a reduction in a just reward, no matter how slight, was quite an imposition. Although it happened only rarely, and we were still given our pennies, there was always a little less elation in the way we lit our candles to see our way up to bed.

By now I was firmly established as the apprentice organ pumper. Not that the job earned me any money, but it did open doors. Our popular minister, the Reverend Johnson, apparently satisfied with the progress I was making, asked me if I would like to be his messenger boy. The telephone had not yet invaded the privacy of our secluded part of England, and as the Reverend needed to keep in touch with his counterparts in neighbouring villages, he had a job for me if I'd like it. If I'd like it? I couldn't accept quickly enough; it was the heaven sent answer to my financial problem. Furthermore, the hours of employment were just right.

On Saturday mornings at 9 am I'd have to report to Reverend Johnson at the Manse. The remuneration would be governed by the total milage I covered; sometimes there would be only a couple of short trips, while other days would keep me going until 1 pm. On a good day I could earn up to a shilling, which to my young ears, sounded like a fortune. And having a few coins to rattle in my pocket was so exhilarating that it gave me a feeling of power and confidence that I'd never experienced before. It was exactly what I

The Reverend Johnson in front of Eastcombe Baptist Church.

needed. Yet it was all so simple. I enjoyed walking. Whistling my way over the Cotswold countryside and getting paid for it, was a situation bordering on paradise. I was extremely happy.

To make life even better, another job came my way when two Bismore families employed me to collect their daily newspapers from the Eastcombe post office after school and bring them back with me on my way home. Once again it appeared all too simple, although there were occasions when I put the job in jeopardy.

Being a lad who loved sport and games, it didn't take much persuasion from the other kids to join them in an after-school game of football on the village green. The only question was, what to do with the newspapers while I was busy kicking goals. When the weather was fine and calm there was no problem, but wet, windy weather whipped up the ingredients for potential disaster.

The obvious solution was to wrap my coat around the papers, a remedy that was only partially successful. The tricky wind blew with such fickleness that it left the newspapers soaking up the playing surface, which, although helping considerably to improve the quality of the game, presented a tendency for the soggy pages to disintegrate before I could deliver them, in all innocence, to their astonished owners.

Those were the easy days. Complications arose when our miniature football ground became engulfed by a sudden squall. This caused a number of things to happen simultaneously. Firstly, while deciding whether to continue the game or to pick up our coats and run for shelter, we got wet. Secondly, the newspapers not only became soaked, but before anyone could rescue them, they started to scatter page by page, in a mad swirling rampage all over the village.

That was the moment in which I came closest to resigning my position as newsboy. I came ever closer to tears as self-disparaging thoughts overwhelmed me. Why did it have to happen to me? It was all my fault, I shouldn't have stayed behind to play, I would never amount to anything, and so on.

But I was not without friends. Quickly donning their coats, the kids went racing down narrow lanes, over stone walls and even up trees to retrieve the wayward pages and bring them back to the assembly area. The challenge then, was in putting together two complete newspapers out of the pieces. That's when I started praying: 'Oh please let the outside pages be there...and the newsy bits'. I could get away with some of the less important parts missing, but it was a little more difficult explaining to my employers how the front managed to start on page five.

It was a permanent source of puzzlement to me just how I did manage to hold down my job. But hold it I did, and what was more important, I was paid for it, adding another sixpence a week to the coffers. I was cultivating a liking for this commercial business.

Although Eastcombe had a small general store and on the fringe of the village on the Bussage road there was a Co-op, most people went into Stroud to do their serious shopping. A bus service took the route down the steep Brown's Hill, past Toadsmoor Lake, then along the valley into the town. But that cost money. There was a backroad that went over the Bismore Bridge, through the wooded hillside up to Lypiatt and along the Bisley road. Because we lived in Bismore that was the way we went. It was a pleasant ten-kilometre walk which gave George the chance to study the cars, while I was content just to count the numbers of vehicles that passed us. Apart from the usual half- dozen motor bikes, some of which had side-car attachments, if the number of cars reached double figures, it was a very busy day. More often than not the number was about five.

Now that I was earning pocket money, I occasionally let my head go and bussed it into Stroud to see John Bottomley, a sort of foster-brother who had lived with us for a short time but was now living with another foster family in Cainscross, about two kilometres the other side of Stroud. As the bus from Eastcombe terminated at Stroud, I walked the rest of the way until I reached the entrance to The Retreat. This consisted of a small group of houses that backed onto the Severn-Thames Canal. Every time I visited him, John and I would spend hours fishing with our home-made lines of string and a bent pin, but despite the efforts of the newly dug worm to free itself from the pin, I can't remember ever catching anything. To relieve our frustration, we used our energy to skim small flat stones along the surface of the canal, after which we gorged ourselves with sandwiches of chunks of cheese pressed between two giant slices of fresh white bread.

On the way home, there was usually quite a wait for the bus, which made the location an ideal spot for the local busker. On one occasion we waiting passengers were entertained by a little old man dressed in a grubby suit and a peaked cap that threatened to fall off. He played tunes on a battered old concertina with a flare that demanded attention. The rhythm and style of his playing must have stirred an undiscovered musical chord somewhere inside me because the music had me spellbound. At the old man's feet was a dilapidated bowler hat that appeared in danger of blowing away for lack of ballast, a peril that none of the crowd seemed keen to correct. A couple of pennies was its only anchor. In response to a sudden surge of compassion, I reached down into my trouser pocket and withdrew my total wealth in my loose fist. Opening my hand, I counted four pennies and a threepenny bit. A quick mental calculation told me that the threepence was superfluous to my needs, so I walked quickly to the hat and dropped the coin in. My action was without hesitation, but after I had done it, I was surprised to find how good I felt about it. After all, I had myself, experienced some difficulty in the pursuit of money. The old man had worked far harder for his few coins than I had for mine.

Life's Unpredictable Cycle

Village life was usually fairly predictable. Our activities and pursuits were governed largely by seasonal weather patterns. Only the most severe weather conditions kept the kids inside, and I was ever grateful to Mother for giving me the freedom to join the others in extracting every skerrick of enjoyment from our environment. There were times of course, when I appreciated my home-life to the fullest. Life was very comfortable in our little Bismore cottage, and although we had few amenities, I was always happy enough and never felt deprived.

There was no electricity, no running water, no bathroom even. No priceless art collection gathered dust in the cupboards, no masterpieces accumulated wealth on our walls, and no Ford dripped oil on our driveway. Yet we lived in an environment of plenty. Our riches lay elsewhere; we were surrounded by wealth.

Our treasures were the love and warmth of a close-knit family, our priceless paintings hung from every window, from the front door and beyond. And all were landscapes that had the magical advantage of changing with the seasons, so that without extra cost, viewings were to be had of nature's magnificent panorama; uncluttered, unspoilt and un-damaged by man's disastrous attempt to improve perfection.

Perfection may not have invaded the kitchen, but charm and warmth were substituted by the bucketful, especially on bath night. While I was still young enough to need supervision, being bathed was my favourite luxury. For Mother, it was sheer hard work.

Out from the scullery would come the old bath tub, while a row of large saucepans competed for the erratic flames from the kitchen fire. After carefully balancing hot with cold, Mother sat me in the tub and set to work lathering and scrubbing while I lay back revelling in the warmth of water and fire. When I was done, she lifted me out and sat me on the towelled surface of the kitchen table, where she dried me down before slipping a prewarmed nightshirt over my head.

Even after all that fussing, I would trot off into the living room where Auntie Flo would lift me onto her ample lap and wrap her strong arms around me.

Although they were sisters, Aunt Flo was a bigger woman than Mother, and perhaps because she had fewer responsibilities, her sense of humour was more keenly developed. And she should have been slimmer, because she walked to and from work six days a week. She worked at Chritchleys, a pin mill down below Toadsmoor Lake, amongst a group of factories that kept most of the villagers employed. On a clear day you could hear the different pitch of the starting hooters which sounded at varying times, so that once they were recognised, it was a useful way to tell the time.

In the season when flowers and plants and trees come bursting into life to lift winter's stark bareness into the living freshness of spring, a surprising reversal of life's cycle struck with tragic suddenness.

One day in the spring of 1931, I arrived home after school to find several strangers in the house. Something was wrong with Auntie Flo. She had been carried home from work, unconscious. I still don't know why she wasn't taken to hospital; all I know was that she lay in bed and I wasn't allowed to see her. It seems that she must have had a stroke, because she lingered only a few days. I wasn't even allowed to go to the funeral.

It was the first time in my life that I had been associated

with death, and it was all too much for me to understand. I had always thought of Auntie Flo as being a strong, healthy woman, without a care in the world. Now, all of a sudden, she had let herself die, and there was Father digging her grave.

If Auntie Flo's death had been bewildering, the sight of a new-born baby was nothing short of a miracle. And what more appropriate person to perform the miracle than the teacher of God's word himself.

It happened one Saturday morning when I reported to Reverend Johnson in my duties as his errand boy. On this occasion I was surprised to find myself being invited inside 'The Manse' and directed to a room just off the passageway.

In the centre of the room a crib rested on a stand. The inside of the crib was filled with a bulge of blankets out of which protruded the tiny head of a baby. Mrs Johnson had now joined her husband beside the crib and proudly announced 'God has blessed us with a son Jack, I'd like you to meet little Arthur'.

Summer was always the season for exploration and adventure. We invaded the woods, knew every track, almost every tree. The hazel nuts were closely watched with keen competition to find the largest pods. During the conker season the foliage of massive chestnut trees housed a rookery of plundering boys.

We explored the remains of an ancient saw-mill at Toadsmoor, with only a few weed infested mounds of sawdust remaining as evidence of a once thriving timber industry. A few holes of varying sizes dotted the area, indicating that the site had not been completely abandoned.

'They be only weasel or mole holes' declared Bill Allen, with some authority. Bill should have known; he was the expert amateur naturalist. He knew practically every bird's nest in the woods and hedges, and boasted the biggest collection of eggs in the village. He specialized in burrowing animals. Bill lay flat on the ground beside the most fresh looking of the holes, and, unflinchingly thrust his right arm in as far as he could reach. Success was almost immediate.

'Dost have something' cried Bill triumphantly.

David Spence and I crowded around him eager to see his catch.

'It 'aint 'alf heavy' said Bill, slowly retracting his arm.

The next moment his hand came into sight; or at least it would have been his hand were it not for the fact that it was hidden under a writhing bright green skin.

It was ten minutes before I found out how long the two snakes were. By the time Bill's arm came right out, I was on the other side of Toadsmoor Brook. After waiting for what I considered to be a prudent period of time, I dared a glance back to see if the snakes had been taken care of, only to find myself staring at a three metre stretch of water. There were fewer wider places along the entire length of the brook, and it took me ten minutes to find a spot narrow enough for me to jump back.

It was the first inkling I had that there were distinct future prospects for me in the athletic world.

On a hot, drowsy Saturday afternoon, charming Toadsmoor Lake lay helpless under the onslaught of a gang of marauding children. One minute she was a serene picture of poise and grace, reflecting the perfect image of an empty sky bordered by a bank of massed trees; the next, she became a beauty ravaged.

Flat stones were sent ricocheting across the still surface, while larger rounder ones exploded into the now disturbed water like shells on a battlefield. A few minutes of colliding evergrowing circles, and the carnage was complete. Then having spent all our ammunition, we plucked large handfuls of fresh watercress from the shallows of the stream where it entered the lake, and headed for home.

In the depth of winter, Toadsmoor froze. Her beauty was cloaked with a more appropriate selection from her wardrobe. The wide green bonnet of summer was discarded in favour of a patterned white shawl that encircled her body with a dazzling simplicity.

She was still subjected to violation however, only this time she appeared to welcome the attention from visitors who tickled her ribs in day-long skating performances. Yet always her deeply scarred evening face repaired itself, and she awoke to reveal the magic of her recuperative powers by parading with all the charm and softness of her former self.

But before winter set in there was Guy Fawkes night to celebrate. In my childhood days nearly every family held its own celebration, using the occasion to burn the accumulated rubbish. The amount of rubbish in our household wouldn't give off enough light to see a away to the lavatory, but fortunately, a copse of beech trees behind our house supplied us with enough material to build a sizeable bonfire.

For several weeks before 5 November, the wood was regularly patrolled for fallen branches and pieces of dead wood, and masses of dry leaves were raked up and carted back to the bonfire site. On the day of the big bang there wasn't a twig to be found anywhere, so it was common practise for those with pathetic prospects to pool their resources, so that two or more families shared a decent sized fire.

Fireworks were more difficult to get. The traditional fund-raising venture was to parade an impressionable looking 'guy' from door to door around the village, inviting the occupants to contribute a penny towards the poor chap's send-off party. The trouble with this system was that there were too many 'guys' being paraded for the economy of the village to support. Unless you had something outstandingly original to present, you were given short shrift. Competition was so keen that parents were known to keep their wardrobes locked for weeks leading up to the big night. A man's suit was a prize possession that had to last years. Consequently, any 'guy' dressed in one, no matter how decrepid, was treated with more than a little suspicion.

But when it grew dark enough, a hundred 'guys' occupying place of honour no matter how precariously balanced on top of each pile, were set ablaze to the vocal delight of the children, and the more muted approval of the adults. And with the low cloud a mass of flaming reflection, the children who had naively thought that just because they had done all the work they could demand the 'box' seats, found themselves rudely displaced from the vantage spots by ignorant adults. Always, there was plenty of action. When it came to letting our fireworks off, it was a wonder there was enough gunpowder left to ignite them. For days before, I had performed a daily ritual of taking them out of their box, stacking them in their various groups, counting them carefully, and then re-stacking them. Each time I did it, residue of a fine black powder was left to be swept up. George and I usually started the night with what we regarded as the least spectacular of our collection; sparklers. Rather than just wave them about in our hands, on this the Guy Fawkes night of 1931, I had worked out a special plan. With the bonfire positioned behind the house, I had to run with a lighted sparkler to the front garden and do a lap of the paths before the sparks expired.

When the moment arrived for the start of the big event, the family sent me on my way with a lot of encouraging shouts. This made me feel good and no doubt contributed to the excellent start I made. Counting away my time, I whizzed around the side of the house, past the front door, up towards the gate before turning off down to the lower path that led back to the finishing line. Everything was going well until I came to the gooseberry bushes. Then I made my big mistake.

I looked to see how much of the sparkler was left. It was only the briefest of glances, but it was enough for me to become momentarily disorientated. And of course, it had to happen at the most crucial point in the circuit. At that precise moment it was vitally important that I should change down and brake hard for the ninety degrees right turn into the lower path.

I executed the correct procedure well enough; the error was in the timing. And with no crash barrier in place to protect me from the consequences of my indiscretion, instead of a right turn, I went right off. Over the embankment I tumbled to land amongst the forest of stinging nettles.

It was my bawling that alerted the family to the fact that I had come to grief. The ever reliable George led the rescue party, homing in on my distress signals and delivered me out of the jungle into the arms of Mother who waited as anxious as ever to apply salve to my wounds.

There was only a short delay to the proceedings; the threat of missing the long-awaited fireworks display was incentive enough to effect my rapid recovery. And by the time the potatoes were pushed into the dying embers of the bonfire, I was well enough to leave the sanctuary of Mother's lap.

With Guy Fawkes night over, it was time to prepare for Christmas. There were funds to be found to replenish those that had just gone up in smoke, and there were presents to be bought.

Fortunately I still had my two regular jobs which, with careful management, would be enough for my purposes, but there were still a few pennies to be earned doing the traditional rounds of carol singing. No matter how affluent you felt, Christmas was never the same without carol singing. Every child in the village went the rounds in all kinds of weather, either singly or in groups, huddled outside a closed cottage door to sing with all the emotion that the occasion generated.

Once again, the generosity of the community was put to the test. Tolerance too, was occasionally in demand. Some villagers had as many as ten different callers on the one night. But generally the seasonal spirit of goodwill overcame most inconveniences and irritations. Only very rarely was the singing interrupted by an impatient householder. Most people waited until a carol was finished before opening the door, and even if there were no pennies handed out, a sweet or a fruit mince pie, or even a hot drink was sometimes offered to the cold and often weary songsters.

One year, I started out on a solo round about a week before the customary start to the season. I'd like to think that the reason for this was an over keenness on my part to hurry the season along. The truth was I figured that the first carol-singer on the scene would be more likely to get the cream of the offering before the coffers dried up. However, justice was done on the very first house of call, when I was brought back to the fold by the door opening before I had completed the first line, and a sharp voice shouted, 'You're far too early Jackie, come back in a fortnight'.

I can't remember the days when I believed in Father Christmas. My earliest memory of Christmas is of hanging one of Mother's old stockings on the end bedpost, knowing that during the night she would fill it with presents.

When George and I awoke in the still darkness of the early morning, the candle would be hurriedly lit before we scrambled to the foot of the bed to untie our bulging stockings. The bulging was not the result of being compacted, but it was the rather awkward shapes of some of the packages.

Although we both had a fair idea of what was to be in the stocking, we plundered the contents and tore away the paper with no lessening of enthusiasm. There was nothing frivolous about our presents. There were table games for playing on long winter evenings, some socks, bags of sweets and nuts, and always in the foot slept a candied mouse, with an orange tucked right into the toe. But in the Christmas of 1931 the moment of greatest joy came when I spotted the brightly wrapped parcel that lay flat on the floor. I knew it was the Bubbles Annual with its extra lengthy episodes of adventure, travel and sports, featuring Cucumber Kane, Fireworks Flynn and half a dozen other heroes whose exploits I had followed all through the year in weekly episodes from the pages of my favourite comic.

George had been equally excited about his Tiger Tim Annual. Between the two of us, we had enough reading to last the winter. The comics were a luxury that Mother never deprived us of, and although the weekly cost for the two of them came to only fourpence, the cost of Annuals at three and sixpence was a small fortune to Mother's meagre resources.

Much later in the morning, when the family came to see how we had fared, our small bedroom burst into life with the sounds of happiness and delight in the joy of exchanging simple gifts. Mother and Aunt Flo, when she was alive, usually received small lace handkerchiefs or tiny bottles of perfume, while Father invariably received some simple accessory to go with his pipe. One Christmas George and I pooled our money to buy him a new pipe. When he opened the parcel, his face expanded into such complete rapture, that the emotion of the moment has remained with me to this day.

In the aftermath of Christmas, the village social life, which could never at any stage have been described as riotous, reverted to its mellow existence. By virtue of its isolation, most of the entertainment resulted from our own efforts, but occasionally the Reverend Johnson organised concerts by visiting groups.

These functions were held in the school, an auditorium being performed by shifting the desks, and constructing a temporary stage at one end. Most of the entertainment consisted of choral recitals, with some excellent performances by an all-male Welsh choir. The school, too, presented an annual concert with each class doing its own production.

It is a matter of reality that events in one's life are remembered either by stunning successes or by miserable failures. One is fortunate if, after a mandatory three score and ten years of survival, the scales registering one's endeavours hover in equal proportions. An analysis of my life's achievements would reveal a distinct list to the negative end. As some excuse for this unfavourable tilt, I claim the acute embarrassment I suffered whenever my name was shouted in public. Consequently, when it was announced that little Jack Ramsbottom was to recite the well-known nursery rhyme, Little Jack Horner, my distress began to mount.

Despite a satisfactory rehearsal, when I found myself alone on centre stage clutching a bowl of Christmas pie, panic overwhelmed me. The words came out reasonably well, but when it came to the last line 'and said, "What a good boy am I"', I was supposed to have been looking at a ripe plum between thumb and forefinger held aloft for the audience to acclaim my skill. In theory this thrilling climax was designed to bring the house down.

The reality was far more spectacular and completely unrehearsed. Simultaneously as my last line faded into silent space unaccompanied by the appropriate action, the enormity of my mistake hit me, and without even waiting to execute the customary bow, I raced off the stage. At least running was the one thing I was good at, but the combination of a fast get-a-way and a clipped ankle, spelled a recipe for disaster. Under the circumstances the steps were superfluous to my exit.

My recollection of the actual landing is a little hazy, but I distinctly remember becoming airborne to the accompaniment of belated thunderous applause. When I regained consciousness, I was told that it was for an immaculately executed 'one and a half somersaults with tuck'.

But the real stars were the members of the Eastcombe football team. Never was there a more unifying medium. A whole village of children forgot personal differences when they were at a match. Even the descriptive embellishments to my surname were forgotten for the duration, although they would be more vehemently reinstated if we lost. Because of the cost involved in getting to an away fixture, it was practically impossible to attend those games, but we rallied to a man whenever we played at home.

The pinnacle of fame for Eastcombe came in the 1931-32 season, when they not only topped their Division but also won the Auxiliary Cup. It was an unprecedented feat which called for a special celebration. Practically the whole village pitched in to honour the occasion. The church hall was hired and decorated in the team's colours of green and white, and a mass community effort was called for to prepare a feast to follow the victory concert.

Most of the performers were members of the team. Their versatility seemed endless. They formed a choir that roared its way through a number of rollicking songs; they substituted more appropriate words to the popular songs of the day; they put on skits, and they told jokes. They even sang serious songs accompanied by their own pianist. Eastcombe had seldom known such diversity of talent and volume of noise.

Such was its impact, that even though there was only

Eastcombe Association Football Club, winners of the 3rd Division and Auxiliary Cups, 1931-2.

one performance, some of the words remain with me today:

> Yesterday I went to the races,
> I lost my shirt, my collar, my stud and my braces,
> So give yourself a pat on the back, a pat on the
> back, a pat on the back,
> And say to yourself, 'I've jolly good health,
> I've had a good day today'.

> Yesterday was full of trouble and sorrow,
> No one knows what's going to happen tomorrow, So
> give yourself a pat on the back, etc.

> I'm yawning, I'm yawning,

I shan't get up till ten tomorrow morning,
So give yourself a pat on the back, etc.
And say to yourself, 'I've jolly good health,
I've had a good day today'.

An hour and a half later, the curtain came down after everyone joined in with the singing of *Hearts of Oak*, letting ourselves go for the last line, which went:

'We'll fight and we'll conquer again and again.'

I was never to see my heroes play again.

CLAPHAM

Right from the time that I could understand, Mother had told me that she, Father and Aunt Flo were only foster parents, and that one day, I would have to return to Dr Barnardo's Home in London. But being so young and happy, I'd never thought much about it, so when one August day in 1932, after the postman had called, Mother took me aside, and with tears in her eyes, showed me the letter that told of my recall, I just looked at her in dismay.

I still don't know what distressed me the most; the sudden realisation that I was about to lose a family I loved, or the shock of seeing my mother in tears. In all the years I had lived with her I had not once seen her cry.

When the day finally came, I felt that I had just awakened out of a long frustrating dream. In the month since the arrival of the letter from Barnardo's, I had been in a state of confusion. Most of me wanted to cling to the sanctuary that I knew as home; the old Cotswold cottage with its cozy fires, steaming hot baths, Mother's comforting arms, the boisterous blow-football games with George, and the comics by candlelight.

I didn't know why I was being recalled at the age of nine while George was able to stay on at thirteen. Nothing was explained to me, so I was left to stew in my own bitter mixture of emotions. It was not a happy time for me. And it wasn't made any happier doing the rounds of the village farewelling the families with whom I had grown up. Right up until the last day I had wished for a miracle to happen that would allow me to stay, but, as young as I was, I knew that miracles just didn't happen like that, and that I would have to leave. And suddenly it was time to go.

Father held me in his strong arms for a few moments, not even trying to get anything out. When he freed me enough to let me look at him, I could see the reason. The stress of a verbal farewell was beyond his capability. But he had no need for words; his eyes said it all.

My brother George was plainly distressed. We had been put together for as long as I could remember, and the wrench was as painful for him as it was for me. He tried hard not to let me see him crying, so he gave me a quick hug, a muffled goodbye, and a wave of his arm as Mother and I started out for the five-kilometre walk to Chalford Station. A final wave at the front gate, and we turned our backs on Bismore.

We were early for the train, so we sat quietly on the long station seat, prolonging the agony of parting. Thankfully we didn't have long to wait before the London train appeared and quickly groaned to a halt. Mother held me in one final embrace, then half released me for a last kiss and a brief hug before putting me safely into a third class carriage. Quickly opening the window, there was just enough time for her to press a two shilling piece into my hand before the moving train forced us apart.

As the train gathered speed, I leant out of the window and waved at the fast disappearing figure of my mother until she was gone. Only then did I look into the compartment, and through the blurred vision of my tears, I realised that I was alone.

I suppose I was met at Paddington Station by someone from Barnardo's. I don't remember. What I can remember is the train coming to a halt inside a giant glass-roofed building full of engines, carriages and people. The clean smell of steam, mixed with the clatter of shunting engines and the noise and bustle of travellers, was strangely exciting. It was even more bewildering when I was taken down a moving stairway to another set of railway tracks deep below

Eastcombe group outside the Chapel. Jack Ramsbottom's foster mother, Mrs Nobes, is the second woman at right centre of the photograph (in the black hat).

the ground. Having lived in the tranquil setting of the Cotswolds for the previous seven years, I found the London Underground frantic and boisterous. I just sat and stared.

The train seemed to be going on for ever, and when I thought that the journey had come to an end, we alighted from one train only to walk into another and continue on through the tunnels. Eventually, we got out at Stepney Green, and up the stairway into the grime and gloom of the London East End. After a short walk my escort opened the door of an old brick building and invited me inside.

I walked straight into a different world. I saw rooms full of beds, taps that ran water into handbasins, baths like long white troughs deep enough to lie down in, swim in almost, and lavatories that flushed with water.

The place swarmed with children, most of them about my own age. I wondered where they had all come from and where they were going to. Adults showed me where I slept, ate and played. I obeyed quickly, quietly and without question. I suppose the other children felt the same as I did, scared and shocked. Everything was totally different from the lifestyle I had known. Inside, there was crowding and restriction. I missed the tranquillity of my Bismore home, the colourful autumn woods, the song of birds, and above all, I missed the company of the people I loved. But my stay at the Stepney home was not for long. After only a few days, several of us boys were taken on a short trip to a new home. No one told us why.

I wasn't sorry to leave Stepney; as a first taste of institutional life, it had been a distressing experience. Now that I was going to a place away from the centre of London, conditions were bound to be much better. Surely they couldn't be worse — nothing could.

But I was wrong. When our small party stepped into the hallway of our new home off the main street of Clapham, my heart sank even before the heavy door had slammed shut behind us. With the light from a pale globe so high that it could have been a distant star barely illuminating the dark timbered passageway, we groped our way until we were herded out through another door into the comparative brilliance of a dull London sky.

A set of stone steps led down to an area of bitumen about the size of four tennis courts, on which a small group of children was playing. The courtyard was completely hemmed in by grime-covered brick buildings, with the exception of a wide gateway in the far corner that obviously led to the street.

We were led across the courtyard into the tallest building, and up several flights of steps. At each floor level, a middle-aged woman took charge of two or three of our party, until, by the time we reached the fourth floor, only three of us were left. The lady to whom we were assigned was more than middle-aged, and yet not into old age. She was in an indeterminate category, influenced by a hideous application of make-up. She appeared out of a dim doorway like an apparition, her small blue-black eyes heavily brushed with thick brows, were accentuated by the contrasting clash of deep red lips and unnaturally rouged cheeks. Topping all, was a mop of vivid ginger hair that crowned a short, plump figure.

The woman was introduced to us as Miss Marks, and we were to call her Miss. She would be responsible for issuing our clothes, seeing to our cleanliness, and the maintenance of discipline. In a brief introductory speech she explained that in order to run any institution successfully, a high standard of discipline must be insisted upon. There would be set times for getting up, for attending meals, for schooling and for going to bed. If we followed the movements of the other boys, we would settle in quickly and avoid trouble. Any infringement of the rules, or disobedience, and we would find ourselves before the Principal for punishment. What the punishment would be, we were never told, but the inference that any rule breaker would suffer dreadful consequences, especially breathed from the fiery mouth of Miss Marks, was enough to put the fear of the devil into me. In the few days since I had been away from home, I couldn't help but compare my mother with every woman I met. By comparison to the appearance of Miss Marks, my mother automatically qualified for angel status.

After the welcome speech by Miss, she led us through the door from which she had appeared earlier into a room almost as big as a football ground only slightly narrower. Down each side of a central walkway a row of beds stretched away to a distant wall. Selecting three beds in close proximity, she allotted one to each of us and told us to put our few personal possessions into a cane basket we would find underneath our beds. Then stripping my bed, she gave us a lesson in making it up, after which we took it in turns to do the same. I didn't know about the other two boys, but it was the first time in my life that I had ever made a bed. In the weeks and years that followed there would be a considerable number of firsts in my life. I didn't realise it then, but my whole life was about to change; not just through minor adjustments to my former lifestyle, but to a complete new method of living that was foreign to everything that I had ever known before.

Miss Marks directed us to a row of handbasins at the other end of the dormitory, indicating that we should wash ourselves in preparation for the evening meal. She also handed out towels with the instruction that they were to be hung on the end bed rail. She advised us too, that as she lived in the partitioned room near the washbasins, we could put any thought of larrikinism right out of our heads.

Later in the afternoon when the boys arrived in from school, she introduced us newcomers, telling them to show us where to assemble when the tea bell rang. When the time came to fall in, two hundred boys scurried into several lines preparatory to being marched in to the ground floor dining hall.

As we filed past a serving point, a dollop of shepherds pie was placed on each boy's outstretched plate to be taken to one of a number of long wooden tables upon which were platefuls of sliced buttered bread. The first boys to be served were distinctly disadvantaged, because they had to wait until everyone had been served before Grace was said. By that time, their food was practically cold.

The first few weeks at Clapham Barnardo's Home was one of the most unhappiest times of my life. As soon as my name was known, sniggers and derisive remarks came at me from all directions. For a kid my size, there was little I could do except feel sorry for myself and lament the fact that one particular child should have to suffer the multiple misfortunes that I had to endure. While I had lived with the Nobeses, my life had been pleasantly blessed. Now that I was suffering the trauma of an institutional existence, the first real understanding of my predicament became painfully clear. No amount of wishful thinking could alter the facts.

For some unknown reason, my natural parents were unable or didn't want to look after me. Then after a few happy years of love and security, it had all ended abruptly, with nothing left in life but to eat, sleep and be disciplined. And as if that wasn't enough, I had to withstand the barrage of ridicule wherever I went.

After a few weeks at Clapham, the reason for my recall, at so early an age from Bismore, was made known. I knew there was something in the wind when I was placed with a small group that attended a special inside school, while the remainder were marched off each day to outside schools. Our teacher Mr Dunn, unravelled the mystery by explaining that we twenty or so boys had been chosen to be sent to the colonies to become farmers. I was on the list for Australia.

It was at this point that Mr Dunn draped a map of the world over the blackboard. Focusing our attention on the continent of Australia, he pointed out the names and locations of the places to where we would be going. With the ruler that was his constant companion and weapon (many a pupil had sampled the painful blow its leading edge had inflicted upon the skull) Mr Dunn indicated a spot low down on the Western coast. He told us that it was the port of Fremantle. Here we would leave our ship and travel by train through Perth, which was the capital of Western Australia, and on to the country town of Pinjarra, about eighty kilometres to the south. It was only a short distance then to our new home, Fairbridge Farm School. Mr Dunn then went on to add that every boy would have to undergo both a physical and an intelligence examination before final selection was made. Here the temptation to impart a snide comment about our general quality of education proved too much for him. 'God help the colonies if half of you pass the intelligence test.'

As yet, there were no definite sailing dates, and in all probability there would be a waiting period of several months. In the meantime, the authorities considered it advisable for us to continue our schooling in Mr Dunn's class.

This news to a boy not yet ten years of age was naturally exciting. Coming totally unexpected out of nowhere as it did, conjured up all sorts of conjecture and imagination. I had heard of this big country that was supposed to be all bush and kangaroos, and when I found it again in an atlas, way down in the southern oceans, it not only added to my initial feeling of excitement, but stimulated my natural boyish interest in adventure. Then a real conflict of emotions gripped me when I thought about just how far Australia would be from my parents and home, and even when I was grown up and earning money, how I could ever afford the fortune it would cost to return to England. Yet looking at it from the other angle, it meant that I wouldn't have to put up with living under the dismal conditions of Clapham for too long. If I stayed, I could be there for years.

After enjoying the freedom of the Cotswold Hills, the Clapham home was like a prison to me, hemmed in by dirty brick buildings with only one small exercise yard to play in. And because I had to attend the inside school all through the week, there was no way of escaping to the outside world and freedom.

The exception came on Sundays. Even then, the escape was under supervision as the whole institution was marched two kilometres through the streets to the Anglican church and back. A further reprieve came for us 'insiders' by way of a Saturday morning's outing to Clapham Common. Once again we were lined up in threes, counted, and marched the short distance to the Common where we were released on the understanding that we return to the assembly point by twelve thirty. To help remind us of the time, a series of short whistle blasts would be blown five minutes before.

At first glance, Clapham Common appeared to be so crowded with goalposts that it seemed impossible for any two to pair up. But after a walk around the place, they gradually sorted themselves out. There must have been two hundred goalposts in all, angled in every direction, the bright white uprights and crossbars contrasting sharply with the brilliant green of the grass.

But the Common wasn't all playing fields. On my first stroll of discovery, I found small ponds and clusters of trees that sheltered secluded patches of grass, but as soon as the football players started to arrive, I was drawn like a magnet towards them. Within a few minutes, the once deserted area became alive with a multitude of colour as the players changed into their 'stripes' and limbered up in pre-match preparation.

When the games got under way, it was all shouts and whistles. There were more whistles in that one playing area

*Jack Ramsbottom, aged nine, on being recalled to Dr. Barnado's at
Clapham, London, 30.8.1932.*

than in the whole of London's police force. It seemed a miracle to me that any team recognised their own referee's whistle. But the games went on without disruption. After watching the play for a few minutes, all the old atmosphere of Eastcombe days returned, erasing the thought of any recent problems. At that moment my only problem was in selecting a team to follow. There were so many combinations of colours from which to choose, that deciding on one was a difficult job. Then, suddenly, it hit me. Why not look around for a side that wore the same colours as Eastcombe? So off I went in search, threading my way around the touch-lines towards the centre of the action, pausing every now and again to watch some of the play.

Away in the distance, I thought I'd caught a glimpse of the right colour combination, so I made a move in that direction. As I drew nearer, my excitement mounted. Now I could see it clearly. Yes, there it was. There was no mistaking the light green shirt with a white V stretching from each shoulder to meet up at the front waistline. I was running now, cutting corners in my haste to get to the side-line to cheer my team on. The next hour was just like old times except that I missed the company of the old gang of village kids.

When the final whistle sounded, it was the happiest I'd been for a long time, but the exhilaration of the previous hour quickly evaporated as the teams dispersed and I picked my way slowly back to the assembly area.

After the first Saturday, the next one couldn't come quickly enough. The only other thing that really mattered was my schooling. I had to do well in that; not only for my own good, but also for my name's sake. Experience was fast teaching me that achievement of any kind demanded a certain amount of respect; while mediocrity condemned me to purgatory.

But Saturday was my day — my few hours of freedom, where I could lose myself in the Common with my team. As the weeks went by, I got to know their names. They were a team of talkers — calling out for advice and instructions to each other in a strange new dialect. If any of them talked to me, I did my best to answer them in their own language. My West Country Quaker talk was fast disappearing.

But all the familiarity only served to emphasise the wide gulf between their world and mine. When the match finished, the players went their way, I went mine. I could only guess at what they did after the game. No doubt they had real homes to return to, meals with families, then spent the afternoon watching their heroes play in the big league, or went to the cinema even.

My activities had already been programmed; day by day — it was all so predictable. Once inside the gate, that was it for another week. On Saturday night when everyone else in London was out enjoying themselves, Barnardo kids were having their weekly bath.

In recalling events of my childhood, most of the detail has been forgotten, but I shall always remember bath nights at Clapham. Deep in the labyrinth of rooms that I called the dungeons, were the bath houses. The outer room was for dressing, while the inner rooms contained the baths. And the baths were something I'd never seen before, or even knew existed.

I remember huge round concrete vats set into the ground, with billowing clouds of steam rising from the bodies of naked children. Somewhere beneath the mass of bodies there must have been water, but little of it could be seen until a supervisor's whistle-blast emptied the vats. Before the next batch could be done, the water level and temperature had to be checked by operating small round wheels that were attached to pipes. And everywhere, the strong antiseptic smell of carbolic soap penetrated everything even to the drying room where we towelled off and put on ridiculously long nightshirts. And afterwards, Miss Marks supervised prayers — only now her name had been reversed into the more descriptive appellation of 'Skram'.

Nights were made for retrospection. In the darkened dormitory, lying in a cold, hard bed, sleep did not always come easily... time then for pleasant memories and fanciful imagination. I missed my old bed, the familiar bedroom with its small dormer window from where I used to count the stars in a rare patch of sky. I missed my favourite picture of a lone figure making his way across a field of snow towards a distant cottage. In the half-light of a flickering candle, I could make the picture come alive with fancied movement. I spent hours in encouraging my friend to continue his struggle to reach the house where warmth and hospitality awaited. With intense concentration through half-closed eyelids, I could get him to move... slowly, step by step; but no matter how many paces he staggered, I could never get him closer to his destination.

Eventually, in a fit of frustration, I would puff out my candle and, then, overcome by mental exhaustion, would drop straight off to sleep. In the morning when the light came streaming in, my picture used to assume a different role. My solitary friend was now merely out for a brisk stroll, enjoying the crisp breath of a bright winter's day, and feeling the crisp crunch of his footsteps on frosted snow.

My nights in Clapham were not always so uncomplicated. The dormitory sometimes stirred with an intrusion of troubled sounds. A repetitive tossing and turning told of a disturbed sleep, while an occasional stifled sob out of the darkness meant that other boys were also plagued with trauma. This knowledge only served to deepen my own melancholy. Then one night the solution came to me. It was all so simple I wondered why I had not thought of it before.

I would run away... back to my home in the Cotswolds.

So excited was I in finding the answer to my problems that I was unable to sleep. Finally, I did drift off into a troubled sleep which, when awakened by Skram's shrill voice, found me a lot less enthusiastic about my escape idea. Still, as the weekend approached some of my initial excitement returned which helped to reinforce my decision.

It would have to be on a Saturday. That was the only day the opportunity would arise. So I decided that next Saturday would be the day. And when Saturday came, it was easy enough to slip away.

The rest of the boys had become used to seeing me wander off on my own. They knew all about the team I followed, so no one took any notice of me as I went off. It had been quite an effort to keep my plans to myself; I had wanted to share my excitement with a couple of my friends, but somehow I had managed to control myself.

Making sure that I kept well clear of the assembly area, I lost myself amongst the horde of footballers, moved out of the common and into the streets.

My first reaction was a feeling of tremendous relief at getting away with it, followed a few minutes later by sheer euphoria. At last I was free.

I had made no plans, no preparation for this great dash for freedom. I just walked and walked with the vague notion that, somewhere across the country on the other side of London, was where I had to go.

Even after an hour's spirited walking, I could still manage a cheerful whistle. The closer I got to the centre of London, the more interesting it became. As I whistled my way over Battersea Bridge, high spirits kept me company. So did cars of strange makes and shapes, and big, black taxis that swept noisily past. It was when the tall red double-decker buses lumbered by that I wished I'd had some money.

That was something I hadn't thought about; money. It would have made everything so much easier if I had money for fares, money for food, money for... everything. That started me thinking; there was nothing like actual experience to discover things previously unthought of.

Two hours later and I was in the heart of London. I could tell I was there by the soldiers marching up and down, guns on their shoulders, outside a huge high-walled palace. Suddenly I became frightened. Not only that, I was tired and I was hungry. Taking my eyes away from the soldiers, I looked around and saw a big park. Dotted here and there, a few isolated people drifted along scattered paths that disappeared into the distance.

A sense of loneliness overwhelmed me all at once. Tears welled into my eyes as the thought of defeat burdened my grief. My once jaunty walk was now a slow shuffle, aimless and dispirited. I stopped. For several minutes I just stared at the passing traffic negotiating a busy intersection. Tears flowed freely.

Abruptly, I saw a frantic waving of arms from the policeman on point duty, which had traffic lurching to a stop in all directions. Then with deliberately long strides he made straight for me.

'Don't cry young fella, I'll get yer across safely'. One huge arm came gently around my shoulders. It was the first touch of friendliness I'd felt since Mother's last hug. Taking hold of my hand, he escorted me across the wide intersection with me taking three steps to his one. As we walked he went on, 'Got yerself lost have you sonny, where do you come from?' For such a big man, his voice was very gentle. But in that instant, I knew that my escape bid had failed. There was no alternative now but to return to the home.

I forced a lifeless response: 'Back at Clapham sir.'

'Yer a long way from home ain't yer? If yer keep headin' in that direction till yer cross the bridge, then ask someone to put yer on the right road, yer'll be home before dark.' With that, he pointed me on my way, and strode swiftly back to his traffic.

There was nothing left for me to do now, but to start my long walk back to the institution. The policeman's kindness had made me feel a lot better, and my tears had dried. Now I was only tired and hungry.

But after a few minutes, the sudden thought of a new danger very nearly had my tears flowing again. When I did get back, there would be punishment waiting for me for running away. Other boys had tried it long before I had, and they hadn't been allowed out for a long time afterwards. It looked as though I was in a real mess this time.

It was while going back over the Battersea Bridge that the solution came to me. I'll tell 'em I got lost. That was it then. Tell 'em I bin 'ours trying to find my way back 'ome. The more I thought about it, the more plausible my excuse sounded. It was easy to become confused amongst all those football teams. Yea...I thought I was running late and took a short cut. Only it turned out to be the wrong way. After that, I got frightened and lost myself.

I was so pleased with myself for having thought up such

a good excuse, that I forgot all about my tiredness. I didn't even have to ask the way either, I remembered the streets from the morning. All I had to find was the Clapham High Street. When I found the big entrance door to the institution, I pressed the bell button and waited. The waiting time was just long enough for me to go into a bit of a panic. Doubts crept in. What if they didn't believe me... that I was telling lies? The punishment would be a lot worse then.

Then the door opened and a man let me in, looking at me suspiciously. That made me all the more determined to stick to my story. When I found myself sitting at a table looking across at three senior members of the staff, the questions came thick and fast. Why hadn't I returned to the assembly area on time? Once I realised I was lost, why hadn't I asked a policeman for direction. Or anyone else? Where had I been all day?

And I had to go all over it again. Finally, one of them thought to ask me if I had eaten anything during the day. Whether it was a consensus of opinion that brought the interrogation to an end, or whether it was my pitiful 'No sir' to the last question, I don't know. But after that I was taken away to the staff dining room and given a meal.

It's amazing what a difference a meal makes, especially a meal from the staff kitchen. It was probably the hot food that gave me the warm feeling deep down, although I was convinced it was the warm glow of victory. I was so relieved at having had my story believed, that I forgot all about the conditions that initiated the escape attempt in the first place. All I could think of at that moment was the fact that I had avoided punishment by putting on an act that had convinced the staff of my innocence.

I had come a long way since my 'Little Jack Horner' disaster. In fact, I felt quite pleased with my performance. I didn't know it at the time, but I had just put to use the skills of deception and deviousness so necessary for survival in the institutional world.

A CHANGE OF FORTUNE

During the days that followed my little jaunt, I had to survive
a barrage of taunts and caustic comments about my escape
bid. But I weathered the storm, drawing comfort from the
fact that as I had confided to no one about my running
away idea, I was safe from the tittle tattle tongues of little
twerps who were always ready to curry favour with the
staff by running to them with tales of others' trivial wrong-
doings.

As it turned out, life at Clapham improved quite a bit
after that incident. A letter from Mother gave me the lift
I needed just at the right time. I was tempted to write and
tell her how I just failed in my attempt to pay her a surprise
visit, but I thought better of it. All letters had to be handed
in to Skram, and I was pretty sure that they were all censored
by the staff.

A further improvement in conditions came when I joined
the cubs. Barnardo's at Clapham had its own cub pack
complete with uniform and special badge. The cubmaster
too, was one of the most benevolent men at the home. The
weekly meetings were full of interesting games and exciting
competitions; it was a chance to forget the day-to-day dreary
existence in dungeon-like surroundings, especially when we
visited outside cub packs. Any opportunity to spend a few
hours amongst children in the outside world was a blessing
that was fully appreciated.

It was on one of these visits that I first heard the song *Waltzing Matilda*, and by the end of the meeting I knew the words and the understanding of them. In view of my impending journey to Australia, I had a special incentive to learn the story.

More fortune came my way early in the new year of 1933 when I was called up to the main office. At first I was full of apprehension. Why should I be the only one to be called up before the Principal? What had I done wrong now? My guilty conscience was working overtime.

But when I arrived at the reception room expecting the worse, the best surprise for a long time was staring me in the face. Seated in one of the big padded chairs was Miss Radford from Bismore. She was the lady who owned the biggest house in the Hamlet, set in a large garden which included an acre of orchard. She was also one of my newspaper clients who had helped to keep me in pocket money. To think that this fine lady had taken the trouble to come to the orphanage to see me, filled me with cheer. But that was not all. Miss Radford had not only come to see me, she had gained permission to take me out for the day. When I ran back to the dormitory, old Skram already had my Sunday best clothes out for me, and despite her look of disdain at my good fortune, nothing could detract from my excitement. Naturally, I couldn't keep an occasion like this to myself, and as the word spread, even the taunts of the envious failed to upset me.

''Ere — did you 'ear about Ramsbum going out all day with a rich woman?' And again, 'Urk! Fancy someone wanting to take smelly Sheepsarse out.'

But smelly or not, as Miss Radford led me by the hand out into Clapham High Street, no beribboned pedigree ram could ever have felt more honoured. While the rest of the gang were out on the common, I could forget the poor little orphan boy image for a few hours. I was being taken out by a real lady.

We dined at a very posh restaurant called Lyons. Several smart waitresses dressed in black and white uniforms scurried about in between tables. Miss Radford selected a table in a secluded corner inspecting the immaculately laundered white table-cloth carefully before inviting me to sit opposite her. We had scarcely settled into our chairs when a waitress approach Miss Radford with a collection of folders, and enquired: 'Would you like to see the menu Madam?' Then turning and holding one out for me to take: 'And how about you young man?' I was captivated. From 'Ramsbum' to 'young man' in the space of an hour was a giant step forward in anyone's language. 'Thank you', I acknowledged in my newly acquired accent.

It was the first high quality menu I had seen, and it was taking me quite a long time to get through it. Finally, Miss Radford sensing my difficulty, came to my rescue and suggested something to which I gratefully agreed. Her advice didn't stop there either. All through the meal she quietly showed me the correct cutlery to use with each dish. She did it without fuss or bother; just a soft directing explanation. Miss Radford may have been rich, but she was certainly not a snob. Her calm, gentle guidance put me completely at ease. She made me feel so very, very good.

After taking over an hour to get through our lunch, as Miss Radford had called it, she asked me if I would like to visit the cinema that, she had observed, was just along the street. It was another first for me. The closest resemblance to a cinema I had experienced before was in Eastcombe school watching the Reverend Johnson's magic lantern slides. But this was the real thing; images appearing on a big screen; moving images of real people that talked and sang. As it turned out the picture was mostly singing; a man and a woman singing together and to each other. I think it must have been a Jeanette Macdonald/Nelson Eddy film. It may not have been very exciting for a ten-year-old boy, but Miss Radford, showing remarkable understanding, substituted taste for exhilaration by producing a box of chocolates from the depths of her bag and handing them over to me during the interval. Furthermore, she again demonstrated perfect etiquette by limiting the number of chocolates she took to just one. Nor did she remonstrate with me when I left the empty box on the floor after the show, a solution I thought preferable to facing the embarrassment of refusing them to the other kids back inside. Not to mention the mileage to be gained later in describing to my clamouring audience the undreamt of delights of discovery as my teeth sank deeper into one delicious chocolate after another. Also to be gained was a great deal more chocolate.

When the cinema show finished, Miss Radford walked with me back to the home. She had treated me to the most remarkable experience of my young life, and because of its spontaneity, it had been all the more enjoyable. Now it was over. But there was still a measure of satisfaction to be had perhaps for a week, by regurgitating the events of the day to small groups of interested inmates.

But of all the gifts Miss Radford showered on me that memorable day, the most treasured of them all was the immense feeling of esteem she gave me. In an environment of lost identity, she made me feel special. Not many orphan kids experience it. During prayers that night, I gave special thanks to God for sending me Miss Radford, and for the ten shillings parting gift she gave me.

The winter of 1933 was cruel. A mixture of snow, sleet, slush and rain made life difficult. Sometimes it had been impossible to visit Clapham Common; even the parade ground became unusable. In the middle of this big freeze, the news that the Australian party would be leaving at the end of April, was received with mixed emotions. Now that the time had been fixed, I thought more about the people whom I would leave behind. But it was impossible at that age to fully realise the implications of the move. The only tangible difference that could be understood during those bitter weeks, was the knowledge that the weather would be a lot warmer in Western Australia.

Then something happened that turned the most chilling of Arctic days into a tropical paradise. Skram notified me that in the morning, I would be leaving for a two-week visit to my parents in Bismore. I was so ecstatic I could have hugged her.

To think that after nine months I would see my parents and all my old friends again was almost beyond belief. And when I heard that the Eastcombe people had contributed the cost of my train fare, I cried. It was the kindest parting gift they possibly could have given me. A staff member escorted me to Paddington Station, bought my ticket, and put me on the right train. Not since my first Sunday School trip to Weston-Super-Mare had I been so excited.

For the next two weeks in Bismore I was a celebrity. I must have been one of the first children to have been chosen to go to Australia, and the villagers weren't going to let me leave without a proper send-off. But two weeks was so little time in which to say good-byes, although it was easy enough to farewell former school friends by being there when school came out. Time has erased the recollections of individual gestures of goodwill; that is, with one memorable exception — a girl.

Her name was Doreen. She was the village beauty and extrovert. Although she was only a couple of years older than I, Doreen Mortimer had the ability to breathe life into the dullest of school days. Her talents had long been appreciated by the older boys, and she had never been adverse to putting on a free show in response to their persistence.

She would start with a flippant curtsy and a disarming smile flashed from a face that was turned at just the right angle to suggest that the devil had possessed her. But it was her dainty hands that took hold of her skirt at each extremity, like a classical ballerina. Then slowly ... ever so slowly, Doreen would raise the arms, revealing, inch by inch, her shapely legs, posed to perfection. And when it seemed that there was nothing left to reveal, she would pause, professionally, delaying the final scene just long enough for maximum effect, while her immature audience would gape in anticipation. Then suddenly, with a quick flick of her wrist she would raise her skirt just enough to give her admirers a brief glimpse of her knickers before letting her skirt drop like a swift curtain fall at the end of a show.

When most of the school children had gone home, Doreen approached me with a sweet smile. Although she lived only

71

a hundred yards away she flashed her pretty eyes at me with the question, 'Jackie, woulds't like to walk me home?'

And it was while we walked slowly down the lane to her house, that I realised that I used to talk in the same idiom, but in the nine months of living in London, I had lost it all. It sounded so quaint to hear it again. When we stopped outside her gate, Doreen took a step back and dropping her voice to just above a whisper, she cooed:

'Seeing thee's off t'other side o' the world Jackie, I dos't want t' give thee something special. Something thou cans't allus remember me by.' With that, she took hold of her skirt and lifted it higher than on any previous occasion, and gracefully posed for an embarrassingly long time. Then, letting her dress take care of itself, she held me firmly by the shoulders and kissed me softly on the cheek. The next moment she slipped the latch on her garden gate and skipped off down the path, turning just once to give me a final wave. It was the last time I ever saw her. Yet as I wandered thoughtfully home, I reckoned that I had been privileged to have seen more of Doreen than anyone else in the village.

But I was far too young to understand the complexities of sexual arousal. In some strange inexplicable way girls held an inherent kind of attraction for me, especially girls as pretty as Doreen. But my awareness was limited to the attractiveness of her face; other parts of her body were shrouded in far too much mystery for my comprehension. I was content enough in the knowledge that Doreen had given me a very personal and exclusive parting present. Her intimate gesture and gentle kiss had left me with no great excitement but it had filled me with a warmth that I had not previously experienced.

I reserved the final day for the best. More than anything else I wanted one last walk through the steep fields and woods that I had grown to love so much over the years. I had deliberately denied myself this pleasure, savouring the anticipation with mounting excitement.

As I set out on my lone journey along the slopes of Toadsmoor Valley, I willingly succumbed to the spell of vivid imagination induced by magical potions dispensed by nature's creators in residence. The gentle fold of the Cotswolds tumbled before me like an ever expandable table covered with a lush emerald-green cloth. An irregular pattern of tracks intricately woven into the fabric substantiated its originality. To complete the extravaganza, little imagination was needed to picture models displaying exclusive creations along catwalks that led to the horizon. Across the stream, resting in the wings of the hill opposite, the awakening branches of birch, elm and ash stretched sleepy arms to embrace a refreshing shower before slipping into daringly brief costumes featuring bursting young buds that held promise of superb summer fashions. In the distance, Toadsmoor Lake lay silently holding her breath in appreciation of the presentation, yet delighted enough in having such a favoured viewing position that she grasped long stretches of scenery to hold them close in perpetual reflection.

I lingered long over this spectacular display, savouring every moment, recalling over and over again the enjoyment that the woods had freely given, and knowing only too well there would be an awful long time between meals.

That night, back in my favourite bed for the last time, I asked my silent, snowbound friend if he would like to come with me to Australia. I did my utmost to encourage him, promising soft, sandy beaches and perpetual sunshine. At one stage I thought I had convinced him when he appeared to take a few faltering paces towards me. But his effort soon died, and with it the last opportunity I'd ever have of releasing him from his frozen environment. In my imagination, he seemed so desperately to want to leave, but was compelled to remain by circumstances beyond his control.

In a way, I understood the predicament he was in. My situation was similar to his, but in reverse. Through no wish of mine, I was being uprooted and taken from the people and life I loved for a purpose I could not understand. And to make matters worse, there were no comforting words from George that night. He had been recalled to Barnardo's two weeks before my visit.

When the time came for me to leave the little Bismore

cottage, my father placed his arms on my shoulders, and with more emotion than I had ever seen him display before, struggled to get out his few words of farewell. I could not understand all his words, but Mother repeated them with no loss of feeling.

'Thou has't been a good son Jack, dos't write an' tell us all about Australia, an' when thou grows up to be a man, dos't come back to see us.' This time he was not embarrassed with Mother's interpretation, and when I looked up into his face, it was red with the effort of his speech, and his eyes were moist with emotion.

At that moment, I suddenly realised just how much I was losing. When I had been at Clapham, Eastcombe hadn't seemed so far away. A hundred miles was not an impossible distance; only a few hours away in fact. But Australia was half a world away, and suddenly, the thought was frightening. Instinctively, I flung my arms around my father and clung to him. His big hands were on my head, and I cried. Once again, it was time to go.

Now there was the ache and trauma of parting to go through all over again. There was also the long walk to Chalford railway station, which, for Mother, would have been taxing enough on its own, without having to face the lonely return journey and the steep Chalford hill. Years later, when I was old enough to appreciate the feelings of other people, I marvelled at her strength, both physical and mental, in giving years of her life to the service of rearing orphans.

So for the second time in a year we sat together on the station seat waiting for the train that would take me out of her life for ever. The last time I had sat there with Mother, I was full of apprehension about the future. On this occasion, there was little change. Although I now understood the implication of institutional life, I couldn't help wondering what the future would hold for me in a far-off country. Most of my tears had been shed back at the cottage. There was now only dismay at the sound of the approaching train. A sense of loss overwhelmed me greater than anything else I had ever experienced.

Our goodbye was an emotional mixture of holding hands

74

and embracing each other, until, with a final kiss she put me on the train. For a few moments she stood outside my window, drained of all expression except for a faint suggestion of a smile on her wide open face.

With a short toot and a few shunts, the train crept slowly away, and with the movement, my mother's face slipped out of sight. I had neither the energy nor the will to move to the window. I just slumped into my seat in a dejected heap, drained and bewildered. I never saw my mother again.

SOUTH BOUND

When the day came to say goodbye to 'Mother England', it was impossible not to get excited. I don't remember how we met the rest of the party. All I know is that the five boys from Clapham joined seventeen other boys and twenty-five girls at the dockside at Tilbury ready to undertake the greatest adventure of our young lives. Very soon we would be on our way to the port of Fremantle in Western Australia.

The ship was huge; far bigger than anything I had ever seen or imagined; the long black sides seemed to stretch for miles. On the bow large letters formed the name *Otranto*. This magnificent ship then, was to be our home for the next month. We had two women to look after us on the voyage. When they announced we could go on board, there was a scramble as we picked up our small pieces of luggage and climbed the gangway.

Stewards dressed in immaculate white uniforms took us down into the depths of the ship and into our four-berth cabins. When it was seen that there were double decker bunks, there was a mad scramble to get the top bed. But once we had sorted ourselves out there was time to resume some kind of rational thought. It had been a day packed with incident and excitement; something I had never dreamed would ever happen to me. I wasn't totally convinced that it wasn't all a dream still. The thing that told me otherwise, was the nagging realisation that my prize pocket

The Otranto *party bound for Kingsley Fairbridge Farm School in Western Australia. Taken in London, 1933. Jack Ramsbottom is in the top photograph, second row from the front, second from the right.*

knife that Mr Griffiths had given me as a parting gift, was still sitting in the basket beneath my Clapham dormitory bed. No doubt Skram would have given it to one of her grandsons.

It was nearly noon on 29 April 1933 when the *Otranto* sailed. The top decks were crowded with passengers, most of them holding one end of a long, coloured paper streamer. The other end was held by a friend or relative on the dockside below. With hundreds of multi-coloured streamers looping between ship and shore, the scene was like something out of a fairy-tale.

Yet being swamped from all sides by the emotion of the occasion, I couldn't help but feel a touch of sadness at the sight of such a mass parting. To think that so many people were separating from their loved ones was too close to my own experience for me to be wildly happy. But despite this conflict, my excitement couldn't be suppressed entirely, although it was tempered by the strangely moving sight of people left behind on the quayside, now growing smaller and smaller as we drew away into the Thames and headed for the open sea.

Once away from Tilbury, any feeling of melancholy quickly disappeared; there was too much activity on board that begged attention. The ship was not only our new home, it was a complete self-contained town with all the amenities for a thousand people.

There were so many decks that the first thing to remember was to identify ours. Then there were bathrooms, dining room and recreational areas to discover. Naturally, the dining room became our first priority, and when the travelling gong called us to the first sitting, it was music to the ears. And when we were shown to our tables where neatly dressed waiters served us food that we had rarely seen before, the fairy-tale seemed to be a little closer to reality.

By the time lunch was over, a distinct dipping and gentle swaying of the ship could be felt. I enjoyed this movement; it was a constant reminder of the great adventure we were on. Even when I was snug in my bottom bunk (the top bunk having been commandeered by a bigger kid) where sleep could induce dreams of a troubled past, the ship's distinct motion would instantly return me to reality.

The first few days on board the *Otranto* were spent in getting to know each other. There was plenty of opportunity for it. We walked the upper decks, we played newly learned deck quoits and tennis, and we revelled in the discovery of strange new hiding places when playing hide and seek. When we achieved harmony in our relationships, we invited children of foreign migrants to join us, where the difficulties of language were easily overcome by substituting signs, mime and trust for words.

But for me, the most fascinating passengers of all were the soldiers. About thirty of them were on their way to reinforce the British garrison at Aden. I liked to get up early to watch them go through their paces. Stripped to the waist, they went from one exercise to another on the orders from an officer with a voice like the barking of a savage dog. Then, with the physical training over they pulled their rifles to pieces, cleaning every part, before reassembling them for inspection. The finale was a demonstration of rifle movements carried out with a precision that had me spellbound. There was something about those soldiers that had me up on the top deck time after time.

Despite the warnings about the probability of boisterous weather through the Bay of Biscay, the crossing turned out to be pleasantly calm, and we had a practical geography lesson when we passed through the Straits of Gibraltar into the Mediterranean Sea. By this time, we had learnt the advantages to be gained by making friends with the cabin stewards and waiters. An extra blanket sometimes came in handy, while a return helping of a favourite pudding could only be had by cultivating the right contacts.

One morning, I awoke to a strange stillness; we had arrived at Naples. We watched enviously as many passengers went ashore, while all we could do was to get a glimpse of the city over the dockside buildings. The next few days were very pleasant. The Mediterranean was at its best; a rich, deep blue, reflecting the colour of a cloudless sky. Life could not have been more pleasant.

Our excitement peaked at Port Said after we were told that an outing awaited us there. Port Said was a different world from anything I had ever seen. There were strange new sights and sounds everywhere; not to mention the smells. On both sides of the narrow streets, quaint little shops stocked a variety of mysterious produce in a multitude of odd-looking bottles and jars. Other stalls, open to the flies and heat, sold all kinds of fruit and vegetables. Wherever we went there were crowds of brown people dressed in white robes and many with strange head-dress that covered their necks.

After our walk through the streets, we were taken to a huge white building where lunch was provided. Then a native 'gully- gully' man entertained us. He started by performing tricks of magic perfected with the assistance of his wand accompanied by the obligatory uttering of the words 'gully-gully'. It worked every time.

Then he started playing on an instrument that looked a bit like a tin whistle, but with one end shaped like a bell. The sound that came from the bell had a haunting piercing tone, shrill yet melodic. While my ears were still adjusting to this strange new sound, the gully-gully man whipped the cover off a straw basket at his feet and directed the music into it. From out of the depths of the basket, a dark object stirred itself and slowly appeared above the rim. A moment later and the broad hood of a snake was clearly visible. Momentarily, I went numb and glanced surreptitiously about looking for an avenue of escape. The others remained unmoved. Fearful of being accused of cowardice, I stayed. It was nail-biting drama. The snake was half out of the basket now, swaying from side to side gradually becoming lulled by the rhythm of the music until it succumbed to its complete control. After a while, the gully-gully man, by skilful direction of his instrument, returned the snake to its basket, and the drama was over. That night, when we were safely back on board, our cabins echoed to the sound of aspiring gully-gully men and tin whistles. For a group of underprivileged English children, it had been an experience to remember.

The next stop was Aden, where the *Otranto* anchored

some distance off shore in water that was cluttered with flotsam. Towering mountains dominated the buildings of the town, struggling to hold its grip on the barren slopes of the foothills. It had the look of desolation. It was here we said a sad farewell to our soldiers as they went through their paces for the last time. Despite the heat of the day, they were as smart as ever in their khaki tunics and pith helmets, and we felt a distinct sense of loss as they shouted a brisk acknowledgement as each name was called by the barking sergeant. With the parade over, they picked up their packs, their bulging kitbags, and their rifles, and clambered down a gangway into a waiting launch. Then with a final wave they headed for shore.

Meanwhile several small canoes closed on the *Otranto*, the slender produce-laden craft lying low in the water appearing in constant danger of swamping. Passengers crowding the ship's rail lost no time in bargaining, and with agreed price, a thin weighted line thrown from the canoe to the customer established the medium by which goods and money were exchanged. This method of transacting business made fascinating watching. But even with my limited experience of commerce, I couldn't help thinking that the trader took all the risks as he watched his produce disappear amongst the crowd knowing full well there was no guarantee of his money being returned inside the small bag on the end of the rope. However, trading continued for several hours with little dispute, indicating mutual satisfaction.

Other entertainment introduced itself with the arrival of a host of small native boys swimming amongst the boats urging passengers to toss coins into the sea. Their pleas were enthusiastically answered by a shower of small change pocking the patches of sheltered water, each coin being pursued by a supple brown body in an attempt to retrieve it before it reached the bottom. Each boy's progress through the water was followed with keen interest, and when the diver broke surface jubilantly displaying his prize, the donor acknowledged his achievement with an appreciative wave. And the novelty proved contagious. For the next hour or two the tireless duck-divers reaped a rich harvest from beneath the sea, storing the booty inside their mouths.

Enterprise and ingenuity were never better illustrated. The survival techniques so practically demonstrated by these people was a rare education, and more than an adequate substitution for formal lessons during the voyage.

It almost seemed as though the Aden children influenced our own attitude, because for the remainder of the trip, all children, regardless of language difficulties, played together more readily than before.

It was all excitement on the morning we reached Colombo. An all-day excursion featuring a visit to the zoo had been announced. Hurrying off the ship, we piled aboard a waiting bus that had obviously once boasted brilliant colouring, but now stood faded and wilted in the tropical heat. After a careful check to make sure no one had been trampled underfoot in the rush for seats, we set out full of chatter into the unknown.

Leaving civilisation behind, we plunged into another planet; a world of giant trees and tangled undergrowth where masses of twisted vines created forbidding blackness, concealing unbelievably scary creatures both real and imagined. Possessed with an unfounded horror of snakes, I sought release from self-torture in conversation, only to find it practically non-existent, as substituted oohs and aahs were gasped out as each new phenomenon was sighted. One such sight followed us continuously, much to our growing discomfort. Coasting along bumpy dirt roads, clouds of dust spewed out from beneath our vehicle leaving the jungle clad in a rich red contrasting fringe. Inevitably, some of it penetrated the interior.

When we entered the zoo grounds, the ancient bus seemed grateful for being sheltered beneath a canopy of coconut trees. Happy enough to escape the heat and dust, we gathered expectantly in the shade, and while waiting for the stragglers to assemble, I looked up to see a cluster of large green pods suspended from beneath an umbrella of latticework fronds. They were the most unusual coconuts I'd ever seen. They were nothing like the nuts I had shied at during Chalford's carnival season. But while I was still trying to work it out, the unravelling of the mystery had already begun.

A slip of a lad was climbing one of the trees, his tentacle-like arms and legs shinnying up the smooth trunk with staggering agility. His skill took him quickly to the fruit, and with a few vigorous twists, he sent several of the biggest pods hurtling to the ground. Then with a speed that left us gasping, the boy slithered down the trunk and stood before us acknowledging our generous applause with a wide smile that revealed a set of brilliant white teeth enhancing his pleasant brown face. But there was more to come.

Picking up the biggest pod in both hands, he plunged it fiercely onto a metal spike protruding from the ground at a convenient height for the purpose, causing a jagged open wound. This was repeated until the whole pod became a mass of lacerated fibre, easing the boy's task of peeling away the husk, exposing the familiar looking brown-shelled coconut.

The display climaxed with the performer cutting open one of the eyes before triumphantly handing the trophy to the closest of our party with the invitation to sample the milk. The rest of us applauded enthusiastically. The remaining pods quickly suffered a similar fate, giving us all a welcome non-alcoholic aperitif. When all the nuts had been drained, broken up and distributed, it was lunch time and we were guided to an open-air dining area.

Despite the normal child's unfettered relish for eating, visions of food were momentarily erased by the sight that awaited us. We walked straight into a trellised-off portion of paradise. Around the perimeter masses of mauve, red, orange and apricot bougainvillaea towered over smaller but equally colourful hibiscus bushes. A grove of coconut palms shaded a scattering of cloth-covered tables, the whiteness intensified by the brilliant surrounding blaze.

In the ensuing brief struggle, the forces of hunger easily overpowered the ranks of perception restoring the balance to priorities, which, in turn, precipitated a rush to occupy seats. No sooner had we settled ourselves around the tables, than a host of cheerful waiters tempted us with an amazing selection of tropical salads and fruit. Talking gave way to eating and drinking as glasses were filled and refilled with refreshing drinks cooled by miniature floating icebergs. The fun of the feast peaked when we slurped into thick slices of blood-red watermelon playing them like mouth-organs until hands and faces were stained with pink juice. Eventually all that remained were platefuls of rind and peel abandoned on soiled table-cloths like derelict tanks after a battle.

My most vivid memory of the animals is a python longer and thicker than ever I imagined a snake could be. But the most fascinating thing about it was the huge bulge that distorted its girth a metre from the head which an attendant said had been a live pig an hour earlier. The man went on to explain that the python had coiled its length around the animal and crushed it to death. Then its specially constructed jaw had helped the snake swallow the pig whole. I was glad I hadn't been a witness to that gruesome sight.

Back in the real world on the following morning, a world of well-washed blue sky dipping into the ocean's deeper rinse through which the giant ship gently plunged and rose, I realised with a touch of sadness that this was the beginning of the last stage of our long voyage.

For three weeks the *Otranto* had been our wonderful new home during which time we had lived out a fairy-tale. From the dreary restrictiveness of an institutional existence, a magic wand had suddenly whisked us into a life of gaiety and bright lights; a life of comparative freedom; a life of plenty. But in only one more week it would all end. The ship would tie up in Fremantle harbour for a few hours and we would leave her there. After that, there was the uncertainty of the unknown. Would conditions be more tolerable in an Australian institution? Whatever lay ahead, it was still going to be institutional living. And as I was not yet eleven, there were still several years of that in front of me. No doubt that sobering thought, along with the dismal reality of yet another parting from something enjoyable, contributed to my disconsolate twinge.

DINKUM AUSSIES IN THE MAKING

On the morning of 30 May 1933 the Otranto steamed slowly through the two stone breakwaters that formed the entrance into Fremantle Harbour. Our party had been up since daybreak. Nothing short of a terminal illness could have kept us in bed that morning. But nothing as dramatic as that had happened to us. We seemed quite a healthy lot. We had been photographed in separate groups back in London; no doubt we would be photographed again before the day was over. If so, we would no doubt be recorded as a presentably desirable new batch of migrants.

We boys sported new ribboned gold and brown Fairbridge ties giving a lift to the dark grey of our suits, while the girls looked drably neat in matching grey skirts and black cardigans with black shoes and socks. White Panama hats featuring the FFS cloth badge on a black band was the only relief to the sombre tonings. But whatever the ensemble, nothing could dampen our enthusiasm at having reached our destination. For a group of orphans, one adventure of a lifetime had just concluded; now we trundled off the huge ship with the optimism of youth setting out on another.

A mere hundred and fifty metres from our Fremantle berth, we boarded a waiting carriage inside the iron-clad curved-roofed railway station. Then with a short toot from the steam locomotive, we sauntered away on our exploratory invasion of Australia.

Fremantle Harbour, c.1930 (Battye 20607P).

Two and a half hours later the train stopped to let us off at the small town of Pinjarra, about eighty kilometres south of Perth. My most vivid memories of that short journey are of the intriguing red-roofed bungalows separated by lawns and flower beds. And I remember being distinctly disappointed with the quality of the snow. Out in the country it lay along the track and intermittent patches of it blanketed the sparse timberland in a dull greyish white. It was my introduction to the notorious white Western Australian sand. But as we scrambled with our luggage onto a large flat-topped truck the countryside was all fresh and lush and vividly green. Fringed by a low long range of wooded hills, it could have been a bit of old England. Only the quaint name of the town reminded us that it was Australia.

Moving away from the Pinjarra station, our truck chugged northward along the main South-West Highway for a few

Panorama of Fairbridge – Evelyn Cottage at left; Domestic Service Centre in the middle; Saumares Cottage at right.

kilometres before turning into a gravelled road that headed straight towards the hills. It is impossible to recall my precise feelings during that bumpy ride along that corrugated strip of track, although I suppose like most of us, apprehension figured prominently together with a sprinkling of fear and a lot of hope. But however hazy they may have been on that first short trip into Fairbridge, I clearly remember my impression of the place when the lorry pulled up outside a large tin-roofed building that was the main dining-hall.

No sooner had we stopped, when impoverished-looking children dressed in an assortment of ill-fitting clothes stared curiously at us as they emerged from the hall and straggled towards the scattered cottages. But the most depressing aspect of their appearance was to see girls as well as boys with nothing on their feet. In all the tough years of my young life I had never known children to go barefooted. I just couldn't imagine any greater depth of poverty. What had I come to? The only source of comfort I could find was in the knowledge that at least our party was decently dressed, but for just how long was anybody's guess. Already doubt was creeping in. Thankfully, temporary relief came from a surprising development.

Instead of moving us into the hall for a meal as we expected, the truck took off again, but very slowly as it negotiated the narrow roads of the village. When it stopped, an announcement brought another surprise. The medical examination undertaken on the *Otranto* at Fremantle had revealed that two of our party were suffering from a contagious disease, and as a consequence, the whole party would be isolated from the rest of the village for three weeks.

As it turned out, this latest development was to our advantage because instead of being thrust straight into this new environment, we would now have a further few weeks of our own company in which to absorb the shocks of readjustment.

The first of those shocks was not long in coming. Our big cases with all our lovely new clothes were taken from us. To replace the comfortable dresses and the neat suits with which we had been fitted out in England, we were given an assortment of clothes similar to that worn by the other children. The situation called for all-out group support, and as is the way with children, we quickly overcame our depression by voicing extravagant approval of a mass transformation into the bizarre and the ridiculous. A sense of humour was definitely the best medicine for the occasion. It tasted all the more palatable for being self-prescribed and administered.

Because of our isolation, mealtimes brought about a further ritual that bordered on the farcical. Food cooked in the main kitchen was brought to our cottages in a variety of large utensils and placed on the ground for us to pick up after the delivery boys had retreated to a safe distance. This system worked uneventfully well when we were in attendance, but if we weren't outside to meet the delivery, the arrival was announced in a practical though somewhat dramatic way. A stone was sent hurtling into our iron roof. But if only a single lob was achieved the message was deemed to have been bungled. No satisfaction was gained unless the missile landed at just the right angle for it to go clattering across the entire length of the corrugations. Even a small stone made enough noise to scare the daylights out of us uninitiated new chums; when half a housebrick landed, everyone instinctively ducked under the beds for cover, expecting the roof to cave in.

With nightfall on that first day came a truce. The artillery retreated, observation-post personnel were recalled, and preparations for the evening meal began. This became an internal operation organised by our cottage mother whom we were instructed to address as 'Miss'.

Whatever other duties Miss performed, there seemed little danger of her suffering exhaustion in planning the meal. Supplies were drawn from large containers that were stored in the kitchen pantry. Preparation, although glaringly devoid of imagination, scored heavily in simple presentation. A scattering of knives, a few dishes of raw yellow dripping, some of jam, and here and there a plateful of roughly cut white bread were hardly the ingredients for a banquet. It was our tea. And as if this wasn't enough to remind us that we were back in an institution, the obligatory reciting of Grace removed any remaining doubt. Seating ourselves on long wooden forms that complemented the long wooden table, it quickly became evident that eating this meagre meal wasn't as simple as it looked. The difficulty arose when attacking the dripping. Because of its solid mass, it was impossible to spread on the bread. This led to the novelty of retrieving small chips of it from the floor to where they had ricocheted after being chiselled from the main slab. However, the problem was resolved by rendering down the bulk into a more manageable constituency. In the meantime the astute among us overcame the trouble by the obvious solution of getting stuck straight into the jam which not only spread easier but also ensured a liberal portion. Those who persevered with the dripping-first routine, discovered to their dismay, that when they reached for the jam, they were confronted with little more than a discolouration on the sides of the dish. Naturally, it was left for Miss to introduce a more equitable method of distribution. From then on, a spoonful appeared on every plate.

After a month of high flying on the *Otranto* where we enjoyed the luxury of freedom, delicious meals eaten off freshly laundered table cloths, no ‑beds to make, and hot water available at the turn of a tap, Fairbridge was a rough landing.

The militaristic influence in our lives started precisely at eight o'clock that night with the sounding of a bugle call. The wail of notes struggling in competition with a stiff breeze signalled our despatch to the dormitory. We knelt beside massed beds to recite the Lord's Prayer after which the pale light from naked globes was extinguished, and we were in darkness.

So much happened on that first day in Australia; enough at least to have induced sleep immediately that heads touched pillows at bedtime. But sleep did not come easily to me. The thin fibre-filled mattress on a rigid wire-framed bed in a cold dormitory was a far cry from the warmth and comfort of the ship's bunks. And there was no pillow. A slight upward curve at the head of the bed was the only concession to comfort in evidence. Soldiers in barracks could not have fared worse.

With the darkness, I felt alone and frightened. Instinctively I sought comfort in fantasising about happier times spent with my parents. More than ever I needed them now, but with England being so far away, a great sense of loss overwhelmed me and I despaired of ever seeing them again. I felt cheated, deprived and deserted. I cried myself to sleep.

It was still dark and I was dreaming of soldiers and bugle calls. Then lights came on and moments later I realised it was only half a dream. The bugle call announced the arrival of reality, and the reality was the beginning of a new day, and a new ritual.

The last notes of reveille had scarcely ended when Miss burst on the scene issuing orders reminiscent of the shipboard officer. 'Everyone up... come on, strip your bed and remake it. Then move into the bathroom for a shower.' Fortunately, because of my previous experience at Barnardo's, I had no trouble with the bed making. Then joining the queue waiting for a shower, I wondered why there was so little action at the other end. Being winter's eve, it was not the time of year to dawdle over a shower. Even though this one meant climbing over a cement bath to gain access, it shouldn't have presented any difficulty. And there was nothing wrong with the water supply, it came streaming out under good pressure, although there seemed to be a distinct absence of steam. It didn't take long to discover what the hold-up was.

The water was not just cold, it was freezing. The fierce spray that threatened the bath with disintegration came directly from the fresh mountain streams of the Darling Range, and to expect tender-skinned little English children to plunge into that torrent was asking the impossible. But Miss had other ideas. With the battle commander's instinct for spotting trouble, she burst upon the scene, sized the situation up in a flash, and sprang into action.

With an order that threatened to turn the freezing spray into icicles, she commanded the head of the column to advance. The impasse was total. The only way to go was through the shower. Hesitating only a moment longer, the first pathetic little naked body, displaying courage beyond the call of duty, and with fear distorting his frail face, plunged into action. With great gasps and a faint cry, the ice was broken, and the diminutive warrior emerged into the comparative safety of fresh air with his face already registering relief at having survived his baptism of 'fire'. But Miss would have none of it.

'A fly wouldn't have got wet in that time', she screeched. 'Just you get back under that shower and wash yourself all over.' Back the wretched lad sprang, arms flailing about his body in a desperate attempt to satisfy the requirements of an unflinching Miss. There was no doubt that this resolute leadership from the flank brought spectacular success. One ponders on the results of the campaign if our leader had led by example.

However, when my turn came to perch on the edge of the bath preparatory to taking the plunge, the whole operation threatened to become bogged down. Without even so much as getting a splash from a wayward spurt of water, I froze, prematurely. A shock panic seized me as I realised that when I straightened up, for the first time in my life I would appear full frontal before a woman who was not my mother. I was mortified. Nothing could move me.

But I had not reckoned on the resourceful commanding

officer. Obviously assessing my reluctance as an act of cowardice, and fearing that it would jeopardise the success of the whole operation, she moved swiftly to my perch and pushed me beyond the point of no return.

The shock drained me of all breath; the water was so cold it wouldn't allow me to breath. I felt sure I would drown. Then suddenly I emerged into air and instinctively gulped large mouthfuls. I had survived.

After dressing, it surprised me to find how well I felt. My body fairly tingled with a new found warmth and energy. Furthermore I was hungry. Perhaps there was something in this cold shower business after all.

Breakfast was disappointing. No more fruit, no more sausages, eggs or bacon, no more toast and marmalade, no more tea, no more coffee. But there was cereal. A thin wheatmeal gruel was something I had not eaten before. It arrived with a ration of sugar and hot milk, but there was insufficient of either to make the porridge really palatable. And the distance the food had to be brought added nothing to its satisfaction. But the pangs of hunger overruled any objection to the lack of variety in the meal. After the porridge we topped up with a repeat performance of the previous evening, both dripping and jam being of the same variety. So was the drink. It was called cocoa. Once again it was another first for me. I had enjoyed drinking Horlics malted milk at the Eastcombe school, and cocoa was something similar, with a taste more like chocolate. It was quite pleasant but as usual with children, it was never sweet enough. It seemed that I had quite a bit of adjusting to do.

In 1933, Fairbridge Farm School was home to about three hundred children who lived in twenty-one houses which were a blend of old England and new Australia. The girls occupied the double storied English style homes, approximately eighteen to each, while fourteen boys lived in each bungalow-type Australian cottage.

The site for the village had been well chosen. Apart from the hundreds of acres of good pasture land, it was built on the fringe of a vast State Forest, rich in valuable native timbers, among which several mills had been established. Unique amongst the many species of trees is the jarrah. This rare tree is one of the hardest timbers in the world making it ideally suitable for construction purposes. In addition, its rich red grain is turned into beautifully crafted furniture. And above all, in a country where termites can cause havoc in a home, the jarrah, because of its hardness, is termite resistant. Naturally, most of the construction done at Fairbridge featured this readily available timber.

Each boys' cottage had a dormitory, common room kitchen, bathroom, boys' verandah, and a Cottage Mother's room with a private verandah. It was the occupants' responsibility to maintain it; the Cottage Mother's job to instruct and supervise.

The dormitory faced the east, occupying the whole of one side of the cottage, with the exception of a small square at one end that was the Cottage Mother's verandah. To me, the room looked unfinished. The jarrah weather boards that enclosed the rest of the house right up to the roof stopped halfway up the wall of the dormitory. The top half was finished with chicken wire. Having come straight from England where bedrooms are virtually sealed against the cold night air, the sight of so much sky and cloud from inside, gave me the impression of sleeping in the open air. And surely, the rain would blow in on us while we slept. But what I hadn't understood at the time, was that the prevailing winds and most of the rain, blew in from the west, so our sleep would be seldom interrupted by rain. And to counter the occasional summer shower, an extended overhang of roof provided adequate protection. This same architectural design applied to all the boys' cottages.

A door at one end of the dormitory led into the bathroom. Built in along the exterior wall was a pair of concrete troughs set on a pedestal. A bricked-in large copper cauldron sitting on a fire place was obviously the hot water system. Opposite this complex, about two metres against a partition wall, was the big concrete bath with its satellite shower. A store cupboard and towel rails fixed to the walls completed the amenities.

'Livingstone', one of the Boys' Cottages, showing the end of the building which contained the Cottage Mother's room and verandah.

Another door led into the kitchen which occupied one corner of the cottage and was really a partitioned extension of the boys' verandah. Fitted against the end wall, was the kitchen's masterpiece. It was a cast-iron stove complete with a spacious oven, beneath which, the moulded brand name METTERS No. 2 proclaimed it to be the most popular wood-burning stove of its era. There were many reasons for its popularity. Fuel was plentiful and cheap; it heated the house in the cold weather, and, most importantly, it produced a constant and reliable cooking temperature. The only other furniture in the kitchen was a small table and a pantry in which the provisions were stored.

Situated in the centre of the cottage, between the boys' verandah and the dormitory, was the common room which was dominated by a long jarrah table, polished to a deep red, with matching forms on either side. A red-brick fireplace accommodated a fire which warmed the room for comfortable eating and reading on winter evenings. Around one wall, a row of built-in lockers allowed each boy a small amount of privacy for his personal possessions. With the locker lid closed, it provided a seat for its owner.

An end door opened into the Cottage Mother's room, with a fireplace backing on to the common room one. The furnishing of this room was naturally left to the occupant, although most Mothers featured carpet on the floor. The rest of the flooring was bare jarrah, some rooms requiring polishing, others plain hard scrubbing.

Each cottage stood in its own grounds, enough to cultivate flower beds and vegetable gardens. There was also a woodheap equipped with an axe. A quantity of short sawn bush logs had been dumped on each of the two woodheaps of the quarantined cottages waiting for some potential axeman to test his skill. Fortunately, the logs were mostly straight grained and split easily. Later on, when we had to carry our own long lengths of rough wood from the bush, the wood chopping and sharpening of an axe became skills to be learned.

Meanwhile, Miss was busy teaching us how to light a fire, demonstrating the art by using crunched up newspaper and kindling wood in conjunction with an open flue that encouraged a flame into life by creating an updraught of air. Our assimilation into the Australian way of life had begun.

It was surprising to discover how the simple jobs were made easier, and more efficiently accomplished by following a regular routine.

'There is a correct way to do everything', Miss said, 'and there's a use for everything too'.

An example of thrift was the use of the soap-shaker. This was a simple wire mesh shallow container, about five centimetres square, hinged and clasped to form a small cage which held scraps of soap that were too small for any other practical purpose. A wire handle facilitated its use to whip up grease-dispersing suds in a bowl of hot washing-up water.

Cutting hair. One child is testing her skills on another child.

The instruction continued: 'In washing up', Miss explained, 'the important thing is to have plenty of hot water on hand. Then, when you've got a good lather up, you do the cutlery first. You do the mugs next, followed by the plates. Any greasy cooking dishes are left to last; that's why you need plenty of hot soapy water. And the dryer-up doesn't wipe the dishes clean on the tea towel. If anything is dirty, you put it back in the water to be washed again'. So there it was. All that rigmarole for such a menial job. But there was one good thing about it; there wouldn't be any breakages; everything was enamel.

The roofs of the boys' cottages were made from sheets of galvanised iron. It was another phenomenon. It shimmered above like a silver sky, held up by jarrah timbers in a network of neat constructional patterns. There was no hiding it...there were no ceilings.

At night, the light from the ceiling globe threw the rafters into shadow through which intermittent shafts of brightness turned the galvanising into a patchwork of blinking stars.

And when the rain came, it played concerts on the rooftops. Its repertoire seemed endless. Overtures, concertos, selections and folk dances came to us with a clarity of intonation and a subtlety of rendition that rivalled the performance of a symphony orchestra. Little wonder really, considering that every production was written, orchestrated and conducted by the one great Heavenly Body.

But there were mixed feelings about these unsolicited concerts. We newly arrived British children were accustomed to the more gentle works from above. More often than not, ours had been the music of waltzes, intermezzos and sonatas that had reached us through muted slate and attics. True, there had been the many dirges of drizzle to contend with, but they had been easily tuned out. Here in Australia, especially amplified by the medium of an iron roof, the disparity was enormous. It was all pleasurable enough when a light shower drifted down, or even a lengthy soaking rain: touched with tautology perhaps, but still containing a certain hypnotic quality that held some charm. It was particularly well-received at night time, when it induced a welcome sleep.

Group in front of one of the Girls' Cottages.

But exception was taken to the rendition of lengthy boisterous passages. On occasions, it could be frightening, terrifying even, when giant thundering chords thumped down, drowning out all other sound. And when hailstones hit, the noise hovered on the threshold of pain, and we wondered if it could be the climax before the final curtain. Yet, for all that, except for the periodical wail of a bugle call, it was our only source of music. We had neither wireless nor gramophone.

Despite the trauma of those introductory dramas, we survived. But not without casualties. Many of us were bruised or lacerated about the feet from exposing tender white toes to the razor-sharp edges of gravelled bush tracks. Our first attempts to explore the Australian countryside barefooted, produced some amazing performances. Firstly, there were the tight-rope artists with arms outstretched to sustain precarious balance. Then there were the ballet dancers, particularly popular with the girls. Finally, there were the few who resorted to the technique of a ceremonial walk over hot coals. Dave Johnson even tried walking on his hands.

Group of boys on a hike at the bridge at Fairbridge.

This method proved satisfactory for short hikes. Marathons were a trifle ambitious.

There was enough talent among our young group to put on a concert. Besides the soloists, the chorus line came into its own when we were taken for walks in the bush. The huge branches of a fallen tree became our impromptu stage as we christened it the *Otranto,* and all clambered aboard singing our favourite songs with nostalgic gusto. Then, understandably, we would close our show with singing songs of old England, Scotland and Ireland before carefully picking our way home, dodging protruding roots and jagged stones.

Those three weeks of isolation were not only a necessary health precaution, they served to cushion our initiation to the conditions of total change. Before coming to Australia, my idea of the country had been a bushland of semi-desert and scorching heat. To find Fairbridge village on the fringe of lush meadows and dense forests was a happy relief, and triggered off prospects for exciting exploration.

When we were taken into the depth of the forest, it was an excursion of perpetual discovery. No longer did we walk

99

among familiar woods of oak, sycamore, beech or elm that bared their branches through the winter. Winter here was a mass of colour from both trees and shrub. The Cottage Mothers from both quarantined cottages pointed out the individual characteristics of jarrah, gums, sheoak and banksia. And scattered through them all in blackened camouflage, a battalion of blackboys stood displaying plumage of impenetrable spikes, enough to deter any attacker.

High in the branches, practically invisible among the foliage, flocks of green and yellow parrots squabbled amongst themselves before flying off in quick, short bursts of flapping wings and startled whistles. Occasionally, a flash of crimson and a touch of blue could be seen in sharp contrast to the ever present brilliant greens. And if we were lucky, a disturbed kookaburra would voice its displeasure at being intruded upon, its mate flying in to give vocal support, setting up a cacophony of raucous laughter. If we were very lucky, a startled wallaby would set off in fright, bouncing away through the shrub, so that only a few caught a glimpse of its grey-brown shape.

Sometimes we went to the South Dandalup River. Here it was a different scene. The bush was much thinner, and there were several tracks that led to the water's edge. The river was not big, but the flow-off from winter rains had provided enough water to set up a sparkling conversation with its immediate friends. Here and there the trunk of a large tree lay across its path forming natural bridges which invited the more adventurous boys to test their balancing skills. However, Miss soon put a stop to that, having a greater appreciation than we of the potential dangers involved. Instead, she allowed us to paddle about in the shallows until swarms of clinging leeches drove us from the water frantically trying to prize them from our legs. At first we were terrified of these creatures, but in time, when the few good swimming holes were in great demand, they became just another minor nuisance.

But all too soon our period of isolation was over, and with it the holiday, free from schooling and the regular discipline associated with the normal running of the institution. After being together for six weeks, the *Otranto* party of 1933 was distributed amongst the cottages to join the mainstream of Fairbridgians. Here then, was the start of a new life: an opportunity for us to participate in the development of a great new country; an opportunity envisaged and pioneered by Kingsley Fairbridge.

Kingsley Fairbridge.

FAIRBRIDGE: THE VILLAGE
AND THE MAN

I went into Rhodes Cottage with Len Hopcraft and the
youngest member of our party, David Buck. As it turned
out, this was a most fortunate grouping. The six-year-old
David was one of the few children who knew their parents,
and his mother regularly posted out fat bundles of English
comics. Needless to say, David was enthusiastically welcomed
into the cottage by the old boys and quickly became its most
popular member.

The cottage had been named after the British statesman
Cecil Rhodes, and had a special link with Kingsley Fairbridge.
As a boy, Fairbridge had lived in Rhodesia, now Zimbabwe,
and later had been to Oxford University as a Rhodes Scholar.

Other cottages were named after prominent people or
cities. The boys' cottages were Cook, Livingstone, Kitchener,
Haig, Forrest, Lawley, Nelson, Jenner, Newton, Lister, Darwin,
Hudson, Raleigh and Glasgow. In addition the senior boys'
cottage of Wellington was being phased out because of its
inadequacy, and was replaced two years later by a much
larger building called Arthur Scratton.

The girls occupied Shakespeare, Wolfe, Clive, Warren
Hasting, Belfast and Middlemore. Later on, two senior girls'
cottages, Evelyn and Saumarez were built in conjunction
with a domestic science centre.

A small hospital, appropriately named Nightingale,
contained a resident sister's quarters, two wards and an

Inside one of the boys' cottages.

out-patient department. A hard-working sister attended to countless minor casualties, as well as regularly recording the weight and height of every child.

Educational facilities were provided by the State Government and comprised seven individual class rooms, a manual training centre, a metalwork and blacksmith shop, and the domestic science centre.

But the building that dominated Fairbridge village, standing comfortable on the crest of a low hill, was the magnificent church. The Church of the Holy Innocents was dedicated in December 1931 by the Bishop of Bunbury, was designed by Sir Herbert Baker, and was the gift of Mr Thomas Wall. The original wooden shingles have only recently been replaced, otherwise the building still stands in its original beautiful condition. The massive red brick structure topped with its steep shingled roof guarded by a square bell tower, gives it an appearance of great simplicity and dignity. Its

The Church of the Holy Innocents, Fairbridge.

height suggests an interior gallery especially by the addition
of an overhanging skirt between the roof and the ground.
But it is a single-storied monument displaying an intricate
internal pattern of beautifully sculptured beams and trusses
carved from the rich red timbers of the bush.

Its dignified interior is 19 metres long and 8.5 metres
wide, and opens through a series of arches into an aisle
at each side, while at the eastern end is a large arch almost
the full width of the nave. Beyond the chancel is the semi-
circular sanctuary finished with a semi-dome in brick, into
which is skilfully worked a series of arched windows,
corresponding to the clerestory window of the nave.

A stained-glass window, high in the west wall depicting
Christ as a child, was placed there by the Old Fairbridgian's
Association in memory of the Founder.

The requirements of over three hundred children in a
virtual self-supporting establishment required numerous
other facilities. These included; Fairbridge House which was
built by the Founder to house his wife Ruby and three
children, the Principal's house, club house for old
Fairbridgians, an office, main hall including kitchen, staff

Norman Harvey and Dick Darrington outside the Bakery.

dining room and kitchen, teachers' quarters, staff quarters, rectory, engine room, laundry, bakehouse, carpenter's shop, printing room, general store, and houses for the farm manager, head teacher, secretary, engineer, dairyman and gardener.

There were also the many outbuildings associated with farming; milking, stables, pig-pens, machinery sheds and a large storage shed in the centre of vegetable gardens. In all, the farm school covered over three thousand acres, and at the time of our arrival, was considered to be functioning at its peak.

To operate an establishment of this size obviously required a large staff, not the least important of which were the Cottage Mothers. It was not an easy task for a 'Mother' who normally would have no more than three or four children to rear, to supervise the upbringing of a minimum of fourteen children. There must have been some difficulty in finding experienced women, because in 1936, out of a total of twenty-seven regular and relieving 'Mothers' no fewer than twenty were unmarried.

However, in this regard, David, Len and I were lucky. Our Cottage Mother was also a grandmother. Mrs Tomkinson was older than most, but still retained a handsome appearance with neat grey hair setting off a kind face. She welcomed us into her care by showing us our beds and lockers and explained how the cottage work was proportioned out. David of course, by virtue of his age, was not to be expected to do a great deal to start with, but I was to have set jobs to do both before and after school. She went on to say that periodically she would post work rosters up so that everyone would get a change of job.

There was quite a variety of work to be done. With breakfast and dinner being held in the main hall, the cutlery and plates had to be set up before the meals and taken back to the cottages afterwards for washing up. Both the kitchen and copper fires had to be lit each day and, of course, cleaned of the ashes. The back verandah, kitchen and bathroom had to be swept and washed daily, with a good old hands-and-knees scrubbing on Saturdays. The rest of the cottage floors were polished, with an application of kerosene being applied also on Saturdays.

My first job was to clean the common room with another boy. We were into it as soon as we had showered and made our beds.

'You've got to get in quick', I was advised, as my co-worker dived into a cupboard to get a broom. 'If you don't, ya could be waiting 'alf an 'our forrit.' It was only ten past six then, so we had about forty minutes in which to do the work before leaving for breakfast.

Tossing me a couple of rags he went on, 'You start polishin' after I've swept 'em, and when I've finished I'll give ya a 'and'.

Taking hold of one of the rags, I squatted down and swished it aimlessly around the floor in all directions.

''Ere, not like that', cried the foreman. 'You've gotta get down on ya 'ands an' knees an' put some elbow grease into it. And do a strip atta time. If ya don't get all the footmarks off we'll only 'ave t' do it all agen.'

With fourteen pairs of feet tramping on the place, the floor was a mass of footmarks that even the pale light failed to hide, so sinking to my hands and knees, I got to work. It needed only a few minutes of vigorous rubbing to discover why my partner had opted for the sweeping. Footprints left by dirty bare feet on polished red floor boards required every ounce of a ten-year-old's energy to remove.

After five minutes I was exhausted and sat back on my haunches to recover. As I regained my breath, it gave me time to reflect on the necessity for an equal distribution of the work load. I was in no hurry to resume. It was a further couple of minutes before my friend showed up, and seeing my long stare, explained his absence by saying that he'd had to go to the lavatory. As this sentry-box style building stood on its own some distance from the cottage, and seemed especially popular first thing in the morning, there was little I could say. In any event, instinct warned me, that as a new chum, it was best to tred warily. But right there and then, it came to me that if I was going to survive this place, there was a lot of learning to do.

At a quarter to seven it was time to clean up for the walk to the main hall for breakfast. In the half-light of the winter's morning, I trod that three-hundred-metre track with exaggerated footsteps. To stub a big toe against a sharp rock in freezing temperatures was not a humorous experience.

The main hall was a jungle of long wooden tables and forms, with a sprinkling of children putting the finishing touches to setting the tables. Each cottage had its own table in its own place, with a chair at one end for the Cottage Mother. In the centre of the hall, two tables lying end to end formed one long table. This was where the big boys from Wellington cottage ate, and because they were senior boys working on the farm, they were given boots to wear. When they entered or left the hall together, everyone knew about it, their collective heavy boots creating an unaccustomed stampede of noise.

The dining hall filled quickly and everyone sat at their tables waiting expectantly. A consistent undertone of noise went around as the subject of conversation was discussed. Colonel Heath was coming.

The Colonel was the Principal about whom we had heard a great deal since our arrival. He was obviously a man of stature. Cottage Mothers spoke of him with reverence; children, with awe. Their nickname for him said it all. It was 'Bonk'.

All at once the noise in the hall ceased, as though cut off by a master controller. As I was facing away from the entrance, I instinctively turned around to find the cause. At the same time as I saw the Colonel, everybody rose.

Standing at the head of Wellington's table was a giant of a man. He was a big framed man rather than being excessively tall — although he was nearly two metres in height — with a neatly trimmed moustache bristling in a military manner above a firm mouth, a long face lengthened by a forehead that disappeared into a bald head with only a wisp of hair above each ear, and a strong dimpled jaw. An empty left sleeve tucked into the pocket of a tweed coat; a stance that commanded respect, eyes that demanded attention; that was the Colonel.

In the next moment, the silence was shattered by the boom of canon fire that bounced off the low ceiling and echoed around the hall. A black and white cat that had been cleaning itself, disappeared. The Colonel was speaking.

'Today, another party of children is joining you. No doubt you will recall your own personal feelings of apprehension during those first few days after your arrival. It is your duty and responsibility to welcome the new arrivals, and help them settle in to their new environment in the spirit of the founder of this great establishment, Kingsley Fairbridge. Remember ... at all times ... that we are a family, and as such, we must learn to live together in harmony and co-operation. And, above all, we should always strive to observe the principles by which Fairbridge lived, namely, unselfishness and consideration for others. We shall now say Grace.'

Immediately Grace was said, there was a bustle of activity. While most children reseated themselves along the forms, two or three representatives from each cottage made their way into a servery that gave access to the main kitchen. Here food was collected in large containers and taken back to the tables for serving. At the same time, a senior staff member supervised the ordering and distribution of the Cottage Mothers' breakfast. They could either eat their food at the table, or choose to take the raw ingredients back to the cottage for cooking later.

In the meantime, while the Mothers ate their Cornflakes or Weetbix, the rest of us were downing our wheatmeal porridge eaten off deep enamel plates. When these were empty, they were passed up to the end of the table where the mess orderlies packed them away in wooden cases for taking back to the cottages for washing. This then left us with shallow plates from which to eat our bread and dripping and jam. By this time the Mothers were on their toast and marmalade followed by tea or coffee. We drank cocoa.

The Cottage Mothers presided over our table manners, correcting any faults in our eating habits. Elbows had to be kept off the table at all times, and each slice of bread cut into quarters. Talking had to be restricted to necessary conversation only, although many were adept at speaking out of the corner of their mouth when urging a slow eater to hurry up so that we could get back to finish our housework and off to school for a few minutes of playtime before the bell rang.

When everyone had finished eating and the dirty bulk utensils had been returned to the main kitchen, each Cottage Mother took control of her charges, said Grace by thanking the Lord for what we had just received, and departed. Back in the cottage we hurried to finish our chores. Only after passing Miss's inspection, were we permitted to change into our school clothes and get away.

On many mornings it was a relief to get to school. There was little to enthuse about in cottage life, whereas I had always enjoyed going to school. I found every subject interesting, even to learning the ruling dates of many of the English kings. Now I was in Australia I was keen to learn all I could about my vast new country.

The school bell taught me my first lesson in Australian improvisation. It was a sizable piece of railway track suspended from a stout timber frame, and was struck by a senior boy using an iron rod. The first ringing gave five minutes' warning; time to clean up and wash hands in preparation for the assembly inspection. It was on these parades that we discovered the extent of discipline in our lives. Anyone whose hands were unusually dirty, after being warned by the bell to clean them, was sent straight to the Headmaster. Here again, the experience of military training in our senior staff came to the fore.

The Headmaster was Mr Healey, a survivor of the trench warfare in World War I. He and Mrs Healey lived permanently in a house on the eastern fringe of the village, and they had both given years of service to the Fairbridge scheme. A childless couple themselves, they had been special friends and advisers to hundreds of Fairbridgians who had left to go out to jobs throughout the State. He was a man of about fifty, with steel grey hair that had once been black, and walked with a distinctive limp; a legacy from his active service.

This then was the man to whom the disobedient and the lazy were sent. But Mr Healy, despite the severity of his appearance, administered justice in a manner beyond reproach. He punished no one until he had listened to a full explanation from the miscreant, after which he had his experience as a former non-commissioned-officer to call on. Anyone who received 'cuts' from Mr Healey's cane usually deserved them.

After school was over for the morning, a bugle call sounding 'cookhouse' summoned us to lunch. Once again the breakfast drill was repeated, the orderlies for the week taking the plates and cutlery to the hall in boxes, and setting the tables.

The midday meal was our main meal of the day. What had been described as lunch on the *Otranto* had, now that we were institutionalised, reverted back to the term of dinner. All my life, this conflict of terminology has been a connotation of class distinction. It seems that those with sedentary occupations and those who can afford it, eat a large meal late in the evening and call that dinner. People doing heavy manual labour and whose incomes preclude them from extravagances, and who need the extra sleep, have their dinner at midday.

Our dinners went with the days of the week, so that if you forgot what day it was, you only had to wait until dinner time, and you knew. But the food was wholesome enough and always well cooked. The stews were thick with farm produced meat and vegetables, the soups were full of split-peas and lentils, the curry dishes palatable. And there was always pudding with jam tart and custard being the most popular. I remember too, enjoying the steam puddings and the boiled rice with currants, despite the fact that they looked suspiciously like rats' turds! The one dessert I had trouble with was tapioca. It was like eating frog's eyes and I found great difficulty swallowing it. But there was no option. You either ate what was put in front of you or went hungry. There was not even bread to fill the gaps. On Wednesdays and Saturdays we had fresh salad meals direct from our own market garden. With the cold meat and salad came

111

butter, a half-pound between fourteen.

Cutting the slab of butter into equal portions was an unenviable task which required great skill and patience. The usual way was to mark the surface first so that any irregularities could be smoothed over and another attempt made. Then of course, the executioner needed a good eye and steady hand because, as his was the last piece, he was in danger of finishing up with a wedge-shaped bit barely enough to scrape over one slice of bread. If the pressure of the job became too great, Miss would take it on. But, despite all her good intentions, her elderly hand and eye would be even worse, so in the end the responsibility was thrust back upon us to resolve, whereupon a hurried consensus was sought and a new hand installed. But only on a trial basis. If he proved unequal to the task, the position would be up for grabs. It was a bit like a cricket team really. If some bowlers were below form, they had to be taken off and others given a go. With only two small portions of butter per week, getting a just share assumed an importance almost beyond measure.

When dinner was over the Cottage Mothers walked over to the staff dining room for theirs, while the rest of us returned to the school grounds to enjoy a period of unrestricted freedom until school resumed. That is of course, with the exception of the mess orderlies, who had to wash the dirty dishes back in their cottage before joining us.

After school was over for the day, there was no such thing as play. There was too much to do. School clothes were immediately changed for work and everyone had his job.

The kitchen, bathroom, and common room fires had to be lit. If Miss hadn't lit hers during the afternoon, there was hers to light as well. There was bread to be collected from the bakehouse, and milk from the distribution point outside the main hall. Although the girls' cottages were supplied with chopped wood, the boys had to look after themselves which meant that there was a constant need for one, if not two boys on the woodheap wielding the axe. And of course, wood had to be foraged from the bush. This kept three boys busy after school — more if the wood pile got a bit low. Anyone not having a regular job was put to work in the garden or sent out with a small sugar bag to collect gravel from the many bush tracks, which was used to resurface the garden paths. This left only the mess orderlies who, having lit the kitchen fire, had only to prepare the evening meal. This was the period too, when we boys had to wash out our other set of working clothes. The rest of our clothing and sheets was washed by the senior girls in the main laundry.

After tea it was bath time. If the bathroom boys had done their work properly, the copper should have been nearly boiling by the time the first boys were ready for their baths. If it wasn't, it meant a night of luke warm water. The hot water had to be transferred from the copper to bath by means of a large galvanised dipper, with cold water added from a tap over the bath. Cold water had also to be added to the now depleted copper level. Obviously, to keep a good supply of hot water, there needed to be a really good fire beneath the copper. There was no special order for bathing; it was left to ourselves to get on with it.

This was where the quaint term 'begs' and 'bags' came into its own. It was the first of several new terms I heard used at Fairbridge. It meant to reserve a position or order, and despite its lack of binding legality, it worked remarkably well throughout the school. So when you came into the bathroom after finishing your job, you found out who was last on the begging order, and attached yourself on the end of it and hoped that the boys before you wouldn't 'hog' all the hot water.

There were two other terms that quickly found their way into my vocabulary. A female became a 'dame', and if she told you off, you were being 'jawed' at.

In the evenings we sat in our pyjamas in the common room, reading David Buck's latest comics or playing ludo or snakes and ladders. Sometimes on a particularly cold night, our Cottage Mother, Mrs Tomkinson would invite us into her cosier room where we could sit on her carpet and enjoy the extra treat of reading the news of the day from the *West Australian*.

For me, those nights in Miss's room came as a welcome respite from the taunts and jeers of the older boys. Her room became a sanctuary where aggravation was not tolerated. Being a new chum at Fairbridge meant that I had to go through a lengthy period of initiation all over again. There was no escaping it. I knew from previous experience that it was coming and that there was nothing I could do to prevent it. So from the very first day at school it started.

'Ay... is it true that your name is Ramsarse?'

'Did you 'ear one of the new-uns is called Sheepsbum?'

And that was only the start. Practically the complete animal world with their obligatory backsides came into it. Most of it was crude; some was clever.

'You're learning the right job 'aint ya? When yer out on a farm the sheep will be calling you, Raaaaams... baaaaam, ha ha haha.'

It was the same old inevitable experience that dogged me wherever I went. I could do nothing about it; any objection only provoked further attacks. So I remained silent... and squirmed. Eventually I knew the novelty would fade with familiarity. In the meantime I avoided confrontation whenever possible. As a consequence my confidence suffered.

But I noticed while reading the newspapers that many stories told of outstanding collective or individual accomplishments, usually the result of effort and dedication. That gave me an idea. If I could do something worthwhile with my life, instead of being recognised as a source of amusement, my name could, one day, be associated with achievement. Right there and then at the age of 10, I made up my mind to work at it.

Saturday was sports day, and during winter the game was football. In Australia it is called soccer. Even though we were now living in Australia, ours was an isolated existence and we were quite happy to play the game with which we were familiar. Although the game of rugby is played extensively throughout the United Kingdom, we were not taught it at Fairbridge.

The sportsmaster was Mr Barrett, a former physical training instructor in the British Army. He was a small man of about one hundred and sixty-five centimetres but as physically tough as they come. His fresh face with its immaculately trimmed moustache appropriately tinged with ginger, and his impeccable appearance, automatically demanded respect and authority.

And Mr Barrett got it. For a slightly built man, his big voice had the carry of a sergeant-major's. He carried himself with pride, his back as straight as a cricket stump. When he gave an order, it carried the weight of years of military experience. He was not a man to be questioned. To answer back was unthinkable.

Although he was a strict disciplinarian, he was scrupulously fair. We children loved him. In retrospect, I suppose he was a father figure. He was certainly the closest to being a father to most of us than any other man at Fairbridge.

He was indefatigable. Besides organising inter-cottage competitions in football, cricket, and hockey, he took physical training classes, gave boxing, old-time and ballroom dancing lessons, and instructional games. He had the perfect combination of multiple talent with the skill of management. Furthermore, his heart was in his work.

It seemed that Rhodes cottage wasn't doing too well in the soccer competition that year, so they were happy to get some new blood in their side. Not that they got too much to start with. David, of course was far too young to play, while I was still going through the feet-toughening process. When I did play, I was sure I'd finish up with a broken toe or worse, so for the first Saturday I did little more than push the ball around with my instep. But I was persevered with. The fact that a team of eleven had to be found from only fourteen boys may have had some bearing on my selection.

After the first game I managed to get the goal-keeper's job where I could use my hands to drop the ball on to my foot when clearing the ball. This reduced the soreness and chapping to my right foot only, whereas out in the field both feet and shins were exposed to danger, particularly from the 'no-hopers' who were in other teams purely to make up the numbers. The experienced boys solved the problem of chapped feet by wearing an old sock for protection. A long sock was even better because it could be doubled over to give extra thickness. The problem was that the demand for socks outdid the supply. The odd one or two came from a schoolteacher or a staff member, but most were scrounged from occasional visiting football teams.

As the season progressed and my feet toughened up, my confidence returned, and as I had shown some turn of speed, it was decided to try me in the forward line. Probably due to the ineptitude of the opposing backs, the move was successful and I scored a few goals. Towards the end of the season we started to win a few matches and I became established as the regular centre-forward.

Rhodes slowly crept up the championship ladder, and although never seriously threatening the league leaders, we had at least moved off the bottom. Of more importance to me, however, was the fact that I had achieved some small measure of recognition. The insults became noticeably fewer.

Sundays at Fairbridge was a day of mixed blessing. The best thing about it was the extra hour in bed, which meant that in the winter months it would be daylight when Reveille sounded.

This was the day when we dressed, still barefoot, in our best white shirts and corduroy trousers to attend the morning church service. No one was allowed to miss the service. It was the Cottage Mothers' responsibility to see that everyone attended and there was rarely an absconder. The penalty was the deterrent. It was made perfectly clear that sinners would automatically be 'up before Bonk'. And as it was well known that the Colonel packed as much power in his one arm than most men could muster in two, the attendance of a full house was practically guaranteed.

The church is the crown of Fairbridge village. But despite its inviting beauty, in the middle of winter it is freezing. The cold sandstone flooring together with the tall brick walls, effectively turn the interior into a vault. This was especially evidenced by generations of barefooted, bare-legged children.

Some protection was provided for the knees however, by the provision of small prayer mats.

Preceding the service, the cassocked school choir walked slowly and ceremoniously to their places. After that, its main function was to lead the congregation in singing the prayers and hymns. During the sermon, many boys and girls made silent eye contact with each other from across opposite aisles. I usually day-dreamed about the coming steamed date pudding we nicknamed 'plonk'. I looked forward to it because it was so filling, a consideration of some importance.

But one church service was different from all the others. It was held on 19 July to commemorate the anniversary of the death of Kingsley Fairbridge. Furthermore, because of the recent new arrivals, Colonel Heath would take the opportunity to explain the life and work of the Founder leading up to establishing this farm school. With the Colonel in the pulpit there was little likelihood of anyone drifting off to sleep. Not that we new children wanted to; we were about to hear the story of Fairbridge for the first time. Bonk's booming voice began again.

'I want to tell you today a story of the vision, determination and courage of one man who sacrificed his own life in the pursuit of providing a home and an opportunity in life for children like yourselves. That man was Kingsley Ogilvie Fairbridge who was born in South Africa on 2 May 1885. In 1896 the family went to live in Rhodesia which at that time was a new area for European settlement. At the age of eleven, Fairbridge spent a lot of time travelling in the vast open spaces of the veld with his father. He grew to love the country; it fascinated him so much that just one year later he had a vision.

'"Why are there no farms? Why are there no people?"' Kingsley said. His dream was to fill the empty land with farmers. But even at that young age he suffered his first attacks of malaria. It was a disease that dogged him all through his life and was responsible for his tragic early death.

'In 1903 he visited England for the first time and became aware of the desperate plight of the poor people in the big cities. He saw the lives of small children being wasted while the British Empire cried aloud for men. He saw workhouses full, orphanages full... but still no farmers.'

Bonk paused for a moment or two, shuffling his notes and adjusting his glasses. He went on:

'Kingsley Fairbridge gained a scholarship at Oxford University and studied for a diploma in forestry and at the same time he was active in sporting and social clubs. Then at a meeting in October 1909, he shared his vision with other colonial students with the result that the Society for the Furtherance of Child Emigration to the Colonies was formed. The plan was to develop farm schools where underprivileged children could be trained to become useful agricultural workers in the under-populated colonies.

'At this time, an offer was made from the Premier of Western Australia, Frank Wilson, of one thousand acres of Government land to be developed as an agricultural school and farm, with assisted passage from London to Fremantle of six pounds per child, and a school to be provided by the Education Department in accordance with the State system of compulsory education.

'But suitable land was not easy to find, and in any case, the development of a thousand acres was beyond the financial resources of the child emigration Society. So, eventually they settled for a partially developed property of about one hundred and sixty acres seven miles from the township of Pinjarra.' At that stage, Bonk abandoned his script and taking the opportunity to stretch his neck he ad-libbed... 'That first settlement was the other side of Pinjarra about half-way to Coolup.' Then he went on with the story:

'The first party of thirteen children arrived from England in January 1913 and the first few weeks were anything but easy. The facilities were poor; all washing had to be done in the open, and most of the cooking had to be done over an open fire in the yard because the kitchen stove was so small it would not take more than a couple of pots at a time. The accommodation was sufficient for no more than a family of three or four, so they were vastly overcrowded. In the early years there was an acute shortage of money with which to build the living quarters. But despite these immense difficulties, Kingsley Fairbridge persevered, and with the help from a local building contractor, new buildings were completed in time for the winter rains.

'With the outbreak of World War I no more children could be sent. Everything was at a standstill, and there was great danger that the school would not survive. However, immediately after the war, Kingsley visited England and formed a new London Committee with Sir Arthur Lawley as chairman. That was the turning point for the farm school. Money was donated by the British and Western Australian Governments and the British Red Cross. The financial position improved greatly.

'But it wasn't long before another problem was encountered. With the arrival of more children from England, the farm became too small and the surrounding country was not suitable for farming purposes. Fortunately, a couple of miles north of Pinjarra, on the road to Perth, the Paterson estate of 3200 acres, with a frontage on the main road, a river that flowed even in the driest season and a variety of soils and scenery, became available.

'With the purchase of the property in 1920, Fairbridge set about the task of planning a new farm school; but new problems arose. The national shortage of housing and materials following the war brought a surge of rising costs for which the London Committee held him responsible. Now, with a new farm school to support, the financial position once again became precarious. In desperation, Fairbridge sought help from the Australian Government and succeeded in getting a grant of five shillings per child per week for a number of years.

'With this agreement in his pocket, Kingsley Fairbridge once again left for England in August 1922 to try to obtain a similar contribution from the British Government. In this he was successful.

'But in the meantime, the constant anxiety and struggle to get his farm school established, together with his contribution of hard physical work while suffering from repeated attacks of malaria, took a disastrous toll on his health.

'When he arrived back in Fremantle after his fund-raising visit to England, his face was grey and drawn, his body stooped and he walked painfully and with the aid of a stick. Early in 1924 he had to take to his bed, but nevertheless, he kept track of the many details of the work in running the farm. Even in the early mornings he would get out of bed, walk to the stables, detail every man and boy his job for the day and then return to bed.

'Finally it was decided to send him back to England for medical treatment, but he got only as far as Perth when an operation was considered necessary to find the cause of his pain.'

Here, the Colonel paused momentarily. His last sentence had been delivered with a controlled slowing of pace. When he resumed for the final sentence he spoke with an unexpected tenderness.

'Kingsley Fairbridge lived only three days after the operation, and died at midnight on 19 July 1924. He was 39 years of age.'

If Colonel Heath had tried for effect, he was certainly successful. All through his long story, staff and children alike, listened to his every word with barely a cough or a shuffle of intrusion.

Now that I had heard the message from the pulpit, it gave me something to think about. The man who was responsible for giving me another start in life, had had to overcome tremendous difficulties. Strangely it brought to mind the story of another young man of vision nearly two thousand years before, only on that occasion he didn't die. He was crucified. It was all so difficult to understand. So unfair. I wondered why people who did so much good for others should die so young.

When the service was over, we filed out of the church and walked the three hundred metres to the east where our founder had been buried. In a simple but moving ceremony, wreaths were laid on Kingsley Fairbridge's grave and the School prayer was recited:

O God, who by the inspiration of Thy servant Kingsley Fairbridge, who has so wonderfully made this School, and has set us here to learn and to do Thy will; teach us to live together in love, joy and peace; to check all bitterness, to disown discouragement, to practise thanksgiving and to leap with joy to any task for others. Strengthen the good thing thus begun, that with gallant and high-hearted happiness, we may strive to build according to Thy will. Direct the paths of those who have gone forth from this place. Inspire the hearts and minds of those in authority, and fill us all with love towards Thee. To Thy honour and glory, through Jesus Christ our Lord, Amen.

STANDARD FOUR URCHIN

It was fortunate that I liked school; it was an escape from the drudgery of cottage work and the monotony of meals. The important thing I learned about schooling was that the teachers appreciated and encouraged anyone who was willing to learn. It was a happy combination. I enjoyed schoolwork; I enjoyed pleasing my teacher; I enjoyed attention. And I enjoyed being liked. It was a bastion against my ills.

My first teacher was Miss Silk. She was a pleasant woman with glasses that enhanced her kind face, reminding me of my mother. Right from the start I felt comfortable in her class and to this day I remember a simple poem about a wallaby sitting on an ironbark stump and being bitten on the tail by a bull-ant which sent the wallaby jumping a mile. For a ten-year-old English boy, what better way of illustrating the power of a bull-ant's bite? From then on I made sure to give them a wide berth.

The classrooms were a cluster of seven barn-like buildings situated on the southern edge of the playing fields. They were constructed of timber with galvanised iron roofs, but were not equipped with heating or cooling devices, so that we were at the mercy of the elements. Thankfully the climate is very moderate in that part of the State and only on very few occasions were they uninhabitable because of extreme heat. In addition to the classrooms, there was a fully equipped manual training workshop set on its own behind the other school buildings. And a year after I arrived, a metalwork and blacksmith's workshop was built in conjunction with a new power house, so we were given every opportunity to acquire new skills.

Early in August practically the whole school began spending their spare time practising for the annual school sports. The only competitive athletics I had ever taken part in were flat races, three-legged and egg and spoon races. I remember winning a smart red fire engine once, complete with extension ladders. That had been on the Chalford football ground. But apart from one giant leap over the Toadsmoor Brook, my athletics had been confined to running.

Now parts of the school ground were being dug up to make landing pits for events I'd never heard of before; long jump, high jump and hop, step and jump. A board was sunk into the ground at certain distances from the pit, to mark the taking-off point, and painted white so that it could be seen from a fair distance which allowed for a correction in the approach run to be made so that a clear jump could be recorded. If even so much as a toe protruded over the edge on take-off, it would be a foul jump.

There was no instruction during those early days; one simply copied what the older children did. I'd never seen a high jump before, so when it came to the run up for the leap, I adopted the style that came naturally; it was called a scissors style.

The competition was between four factions; red, white, blue and gold, with each faction having its leader whose job it was to absorb the *Otranto* party into their ranks by means of a ballot. Mr Healey organised everything. He introduced the leaders to each class at the same time advising us new arrivals of our factions. I was in blue faction with Harry Lucas as my leader, and when I saw this powerfully-built big boy standing in front of the class, I felt well pleased to be in his team.

A few days later Mr Healey went the rounds of the classrooms again to complete a register of competitors for all events. He explained that there were three classes of competition depending on a child's age; sub-junior, junior and senior. Because I wasn't to be eleven until after the events, I was to compete as a sub- junior. I nominated for every event that was available.

Excitement grew as the annual sports day drew nearer. Mr Healey used his senior pupils to prepare the sports ground for the events. Eight running lanes were marked by string lines, the start and finish lines had to be measured and marked, and new jump pits had to be dug with rakes at hand to erase old landing marks. The teachers would be the marshals and stewards preparing competitors for their events, measuring distances jumped, and times run. Some of them would be the judges. It was going to be a big day for Fairbridge.

When the big day did arrive, it was impossible not to be caught up with the exciting atmosphere of the occasion. Somehow, anyone who was not competing had managed to scrounge some sort of material in the four faction colours and made them into rosettes or other forms of decoration in support of their team. Last- minute dressings were applied to stone bruises, chapped feet or stubbed toes.

Mr Healey gave the word — and the word was 'go'! All day the battle raged, first one faction gained the ascendency, then another. It was obvious there was a well-contested programme under way. When a truce was called for lunch, there was time for reckoning. And I had every reason to be pleased with my performance thus far. I had won my three events of the morning; the 50 yards, the 220 yards and the high jump.

But the most satisfying of all was when Harry Lucas put his hand on my shoulder and said, 'Congratulations Jack. If you keep going the way you are, you've got a good chance to win the medal.'

'What medal?' I thought. I hadn't heard anything about a medal. I was happy enough to win a few events, and perhaps help blue faction to win the shield.

For once in my life I had difficulty eating my dinner. It wasn't so much that the success had gone to my head.

On the contrary, it had attacked my stomach. It was so churned up as the result of so much popularity coming my way, that I couldn't force it to accept the food. It seemed that extraordinary decisions accompanied unprecedented events when even Miss excused me for not getting through my meal. Rhodes had never had a potential champion athlete before. But my uneaten food was not wasted. The other kids saw to it that nothing went back to the kitchen. Dinnertime usually went all too quickly. Today it seemed to last for ever. There were three more events to tackle in the afternoon and I couldn't bear the waiting. The tension became almost unbearable when Miss announced that she was coming to cheer me on.

And fortunately the afternoon went very well for the blue team and especially for me. I won the high jump, the hop, step and jump and throwing the cricket ball. It had been a clean sweep. I had won the sub-junior medal and blue faction had won the shield. At last I had made a name for myself, and it had not been derogatory. But I would have to wait for my medal. It was the tradition of the school to make the presentations at Fairbridge's Annual Spring Show in mid-October.

A few days later, Mr Healey announced the names of the squad that would represent Fairbridge at the inter-school sports meeting in Pinjarra. When my name was called out I was ecstatic. To be chosen to represent the school was an honour beyond my wildest expectations.

In the two weeks leading up to the clash of local schools, Mr Healey gave the squad every encouragement. He personally supervised training sessions and even permitted some of the other teachers to help in our preparation. We felt we had a good team, but of course we had no idea of how strong the other schools were, although we suspected that Pinjarra and Mandurah would provide the stiffest opposition. But whatever the outcome, I was looking forward to the competition because it would give me my first opportunity to see and meet other ordinary Australian school children.

After the thrill of our own sports day, the inter-school

sports brought me back to earth. From the very first event, it was obvious that the competition was going to be pretty keen.

The venue was on the Pinjarra Race Track which immediately won approval from the Fairbridge team because of its splendid grass surface. In contrast to the uneven, uncut surface of our training ground, here the grass was of even growth and immaculately cut which would feel very comfortable underneath our bare feet.

If I had expected to find any marked differences in the appearance of the other school children, I was soon to find out that there was none. They were a trifle more tanned perhaps, but they wore similar clothes to us, athletic tops and shorts. But most surprising of all was to see so many of them barefooted like ourselves. So after only a few minutes of integration, the only way of identification was the school colour pinned to each child's singlet.

As the competition progressed, it was evident that the fight for the champion school would indeed be between Mandurah and Pinjarra. A huge blackboard resting on a tall easel gave the progressive scores and it was interesting to discover the names of the other participating schools, several of which ended in 'up'. There was Dwellingup, Coolup, and North Dandalup, with the remaining team coming from Waroona.

But in the end it was Pinjarra that came out the winner, and despite the fact that Fairbridge was outclassed in most events, we finished well off the bottom. And, although I didn't win a race, I had the experience of understanding the disappointment of losing.

Before being chosen as a suitable child for the Fairbridge scheme, everyone of us had to pass an intelligence test, which, no doubt, the selection panel deemed adequate. Over the years, there were occasions when a child's pattern of behaviour came under scrutiny, and in extreme cases some were sent back as being unsuitable. I don't know if my intelligence was ever seriously questioned, but one particular incident would have qualified me for instant repatriation.

It must have happened on a Saturday morning because we weren't at school. A few of us Rhodes boys were engaged in the healthy pastime of harassing big black ants on the one suitable piece of dirty sand in the back garden. The rest of the yard was far too clean to make life interesting, and in fact, when the supply of ants ran out, and a boring morning seemed inevitable, I made a significant discovery — a three inch nail. But this nail must have lain in the ground ever since the cottage was built, because it had deteriorated into a length of burnt-bronze and rusty brown metal.

For no apparent reason, I stood this potentially lethal object on its head and, holding it with one hand, used the other to pile on the sand until it was completely buried. All that was visible was a neat cone-shaped mound of dirty sand with not a trace of its hidden danger. The Viet-Cong could not have devised a more deadly trap.

But having constructed the device was only half the exercise; it had to be tested. As I had not attempted to conceal my activity, I was afraid that the element of surprise had been surrendered, and to find a volunteer now would be difficult. The question of testing my own weapon did not come under serious consideration. Then in a moment of inspiration, I announced, 'Anyone jumping on that will get a big surprise'.

To my astonishment this challenging invitation brought an instant response. It was obvious that David Buck had been engrossed in his own activity, because, without a moment's hesitation he scrambled to his feet, leaped into the air, and landed square on the target.

I do not know which was the more bewildering; the fleeting realisation that my gadget worked, or David's terrible yell of anguish. To this day, I can still hear the fading cries of David as he was carried away to the hospital, while I awaited a deserving punishment.

September and October bring gale-force winds sometimes accompanied by drenching rains to the south-western coast of Western Australia. They are the Roaring Forties, winds

127

that sweep along the 40th parallel from off the coast of Africa, and which were used to advantage by the tall ships on their way from Europe to the East Indies.

Whether it was the force of one of these gales, or a gripping pain in my stomach that awakened me on a particularly tempestuous night I'll never know. What I did know was that I was suddenly and urgently in need of a visit to the lavatory, but that meant a walk in the pouring rain to the little house in the back garden. It wasn't only the frightening blackness of the night that had me hesitating. There were all the other perils that lurked in the garden. Before I had left England, well- meaning but largely ignorant people had warned me about the dangers of redback spiders and funnel web spiders, and the scorpions and all the other nasties that Australia was full of. And worst of all was the bite of the miniature blue-tongued crocodile that was known never to release its grip on a tasty morsel.

Just the thought of the consequences of an attack in the blackness of the lavatory was enough to turn me into a quivering jelly. My imagination ran riot. Although I was still only a small boy, I knew enough to know that the 'tackle' a lad had was going to be of some importance when he grew up. The English doctor had even treated that part of me with exaggerated care. So I was far too young to be sacrificed.

To make matters worse, the ferocity of the rain was now threatening to pierce the iron roof. My heartbeat quickened … my breathing stopped … my abdominal pain worsened. I had to do something, immediately.

Throwing all caution to the wind, I leapt out of bed and succumbed to the instinct of self-preservation. Then, taking care not to collide with the other beds, I hurried as fast as I dared to a position between the most distant beds. Frantically tearing off my pyjama pants, I squatted down just in time to avoid collecting the incriminating evidence. Now the forces of nature took over, and nature was at her most impressive best. In just one uncontrollably swift motion it was done. But fear of discovery disempowered all other emotion as I crept furtively back to my bed, slipped my pants back on and disappeared beneath the sheets.

Gradually some semblance of rational thought returned, the first of which was an immense feeling of relief. But it was followed very quickly by guilty spasms of doubt and fresh fears. What if I had been seen? How could it be explained? What terrible punishment awaited me? Through all this self-torture, one consolatory thought begged to be heard and I gladly gave it rein. How could I have possibly been heard with so much noise going on? An elephant could have trumpeted that night and still not have been discovered. All I could do now was to let myself be dulled by the hypnotic sound of rain and eventually drift into a troubled sleep.

Reveille the next morning brought with it an extraordinary turn of events. Although the storm had abated, the wind was still strong enough to send the bugle's call scurrying over the village in fitful surges. For a few fleeting seconds the normal bustle of bed-making activity filled the air till suddenly, a strange wail clashed with the note of the bugle and brought everyone to a standstill wondering whatever could have made such a weird noise.

It couldn't possibly have been the result of the bugler's aberration; no musical instrument ever made could have produced that sound. Only the human voice was capable of such a cry — a cry of horror, of anguish, of revulsion ...

The evidence had been sighted.

I was sorry for Mrs Tomkinson. If it had been any other Cottage Mother it wouldn't have bothered me, but to see her burst through the door from her verandah and then recoil in shock as she followed the direction of an accusing finger, was enough for me to almost volunteer an instant confession. And I very nearly succumbed to this insane action when I could get near enough to witness the result of my midnight meander.

There on the polished boards, resting in relaxed mode and looking remarkably like a plasticine copy of a coiled brown snake, was the fruit of my labour. A small head-shaped portion separated from the body, as though deposited in a nervous spasm, perched precariously on top of the coils.

From the gathered audience there were gasps all round.

But from abhorrence or admiration it was difficult to tell. Naturally, the satisfaction I felt for my achievement, interpreted the response as begrudging applause disguised as pungent disdain. The other boys certainly had cause to be jealous, while I strove to temper an inward admiration to an outward display of simple satisfaction.

To my eternal shame I remained silent. So did the rest of the cottage as they recovered from the initial shock and stood around like mourners at a funeral gazing at the coffin for the last time.

Reluctantly removing my stare from the grave, I risked taking a discrete glance to see how Miss was reacting. Straight away, I wished that I hadn't. It was plainly evident that she was under extreme strain. Her normally kind face was now creased in suffering and her mouth twitched with the struggle for a verbal response. Finally, she spoke: 'The boy who did ... er ... this, must obviously be ill; all he needs do is to clean it up and no further action will be taken.'

How typical it was of Miss to take this generous attitude. How could anyone fail to respond to such a reasonable request? Surely, now that such leniency had been shown, the culprit would own up and get on with the cleaning up. Any ordinary boy would.

But still the culprit remained silent. As he struggled with his conscience he reminded himself of the reasons why he couldn't own up. An ordinary boy usually had an ordinary name. He was an ordinary boy but with an extraordinary name and who was never allowed to forget it. He might get an occasional reprieve now and then; as a matter of fact he had just earned himself a respite from jeering taunts that his name provided. Imagine the consequences of owning up to it. In one awful moment he could picture the first impact it would have ...

'Did you hear about Ramsbottom shitting on the floor?' Imagine the barrage of derision that would provoke. There would be no end to it. Hastily, he pushed the image clear out of his head, and he was brought back to reality by the sound of a voice.

'Very well then', Miss said resignedly, 'as the culprit did

130

not use any paper, I shall examine all pyjama pants. Stand by your beds.'

Panic stations again. I hadn't thought of that. I must be found out now. There must be more than enough evidence to give me away. But all I could do was to wait for the inevitable.

The inspection started and so did the agony of waiting. Fourteen pairs of pants were laid out on the end of beds, and mine was about half way. The closer Miss got, the greater grew my anguish. Surely she would see guilt written all over my face. Why, oh why, couldn't I just own up and put myself out of my misery? I hesitated ... then before I could do anything else, she was at my side with my pyjamas in her hands. I hardly dared to look, yet when I did find the courage to glance in her direction fearing the worst, my glance expanded into a stare of incredibility. Apparently so forceful had been my bowel action, that there was hardly a trace of evidence to be seen. In fact, Miss was so disinterested in my pyjama pants that she quickly moved on to the next bed. If Miss had only spent a little longer with me, she most certainly would have seen the look of relief on my face. But my luck held. Someone further along had claimed her attention.

It was Charlie Sparling who saved me. Poor Charlie definitely hadn't committed the crime, yet he looked certain to get the blame. When you're down on your luck, its amazing how misfortune has a habit of compounding through uncontrollable circumstances. This day, Charlie was a cruel victim of circumstance. For the past few days, he had suffered from flatulence which he relieved at night by 'letting off' in bed where the sound was muted by the blankets. It was all in the timing really. A week earlier and he would have had a clean sheet; or at least pyjamas. It was enough to convince Miss that he was the guilty one. And I was really happy for Charlie's sake when Miss kept her word and didn't give him extra punishment for not owning up.

All he had to do was to clean up the mess.

In the green months from May to October Fairbridge village

fairly blossomed with colour and there were the best reasons in the world for it to do so. In the first place, the village had been well-sited on the fringe of the Darling Scarp through which flowed a year-round supply of the sweet fresh water of the South Dandalup River. In one of its deepest holes behind the church, a pipeline fed water into a huge storage tank that sat on the crest of a hill in a commanding position. Fairbridge's own engine room supplied the power to the riverside pump that kept the tank full. So even in the hottest weather there was plenty of water available to maintain each cottage garden in a good condition. All that was needed was effort, and there was no shortage of potential with all cottages full. That left only incentive. This was provided when the Fairbridge Annual Spring Show was held. Organised by Mr and Mrs Healey, and with the co-operation of most of the staff, it was one of the highlights of each year.

Busy little hands pulled up weeds, trimmed lawns and raked- over gravelled paths in a last-minute effort to gain the judge's approval. The best produce and the choicest blooms were already being prepared for display and judging later in the day. The normally austere dining hall was almost unrecognisable with tables hidden under carpets of flora, masses of vegetables and an impressive variety of art and needlework. Not since Eastcombe's Harvest Festival had I seen such a display. But here in Australia there was far more variety.

On the previous evening, parties of children had roamed the hills in search of wildflowers and most had returned with a wide selection including several species of orchids. And even though I had been at Fairbridge for only a few months, I had already learnt the names of most of them. By far the most interesting were the spider orchids with their long spindly 'legs', but the donkey, the wax, and all the others were almost equally attractive. And of course the bush was alive with the unique long-stemmed kangaroo paws, and these featured prominently in all the mixed wild-flower arrangements.

Always at hand ready to give their services to the farm school were the old established families of Pinjarra — the

Small group with one of the Girls' Cottages in the background.

Patersons and the McLartys. It was inevitable that Pinjarra and Fairbridge enjoyed a special relationship, and these pioneer families became almost an extension of Fairbridge itself. It was no surprise then, to know that members of these families did most of the judging.

And as soon as the judging was over, a wave of eager exhibitors together with the general crowd swamped the hall to see who had taken out the prizes and to view the entire display. The excitement was contagious; even the non-competitors became infected with the thrill of the winners.

But towards the middle of the afternoon everyone had a chance to recuperate during the official opening ceremony in which several speeches were made. As necessary as they were, they still taxed the patience of small children eager to resume their noisy revelry. Eventually, after the last speaker had been enthusiastically applauded, it was time for the presentation of trophies. There were cups for gardening (both boys and girls), most improved garden, sewing, handicrafts, cooking, sports, football, cricket and sportsmanship. By the time the medals were presented, I was churning with excitement. And when the announcement came I could hardly believe it was happening.

'The winner of the sub-junior medal is Jack Ramsbottom.' Bursting with pride I walked quickly up the few steps on to the dias to have my hand shaken and the presentation made.

'Well done Ramsbottom, see to it that you go on to represent Australia one day.'

'Thankyou sir', I mumbled, anxious to rejoin the crowd and have a good look at my medal. But even as I was returning, I was conscious of the generous applause that accompanied me. More pleasantly surprising however, was the fact that at the mention of my name, there was not one laugh or derision. As for the presenter's comments — I did go on to represent Australia, but not in a sporting fixture.

Although our own show was over, there was still plenty of endeavour for the enthusiasts, no doubt supervised and arranged by Mrs Healey and her helpers. And their efforts certainly paid dividends. At the 1933 Western Australian Wildflower Association's show in Perth, Fairbridge won the Championship Cup for the fourth consecutive year. And an entry in *The Fairbridgian*, the farm school's own magazine, reads, 'Murray District Show. As usual we won the Fawcett Gold Medal — being the winner of the greatest number of prizes.'

With October nearly finished, I looked forward to Guy Fawkes night. With all the wood that was available in the bush, I expected to see preparations to build a huge bonfire. And when I asked Miss where I could buy my fireworks, she gave me such an incredible look that I put all thoughts of fireworks out of my head. As a compensatory placebo, I asked her permission to spend some of my money at the village store. It was no good going to the store even if you had some money hidden away, because you wouldn't be served without the obligatory note of permission. This latest request was met with a full-blooded verbal assault. 'What do you want to spend your money on lollies for?' Miss shouted. 'You've got Mandurah coming up straight after Christmas; you'll want all your money for that.'

Her insistence in using the childish Australian term 'lolly' upset me more than the apparent refusal, but she relented when she saw the hurt in my eyes, and after finding fountain pen and note-paper, she magnanimously wrote the permit: 'This gives authority for Jack Ramsbottom to spend one penny', signed Ruth Tomkinson. And the note was dated. There was no doubt about it; Miss should have been in charge of the National Purse.

But during the years of the Great Depression, one penny to a desperate family was a significant sum. Three more, and it meant a loaf of bread. To an orphan child, it was a small fortune.

Most of the pleasure in spending it was in the selection. Miss Heath, as storekeeper, would display practically the entire confectionary stock.

She stood on the other side of the counter towering almost

as tall as her soldier father. But that was as far as the similarity went. Her wide open face reflected a special kindness which she displayed along with practically the whole confectionary stock, and she patiently explained the complete range of prices and the permutations of choice. With directional waves of her big hands, she went into her sales talk.

'This is the ha'penny stick box; the boiled lollies are six a penny; the toffees and licorice allsorts are four a penny, and the all-day suckers are two a penny. Or you may have a ha'penny stick with two of these, or three of those, or one gobstopper', reverting to the term she knew we used.

Having thoroughly confused you with this dazzling display of options she never hurried you. She understood the importance of the decision and gave you plenty of time to choose. Or if she was busy, she'd say with a sweep of her hand, 'You have a look over these Ramsbottom, and give me a call when you have decided. I have work to do.'

The decision was not easy; it had to be well thought out. The licorice were good value and tasted nice; the toffees had that lovely caramel flavour, and would last twice as long if you sucked them and didn't chew them. Then there was the gobstopper; one could last two or three days if you were careful. And it was fascinating to see it change colour every time you looked at it. Another advantage with the gobstopper was you could always save some for another day if you wanted to; or suck it down to marble size and you still had enough to swap for, say, half an apple or two cores. I was talking to myself now … yair, I think I'll have a gobstopper … now what else will I get? And the procrastination went on …

Finally, I settled for the toffees and gave Miss Heath a call. After handing over my hot little penny, she gave me my selection in a small white paper bag and off I trotted feeling pleased with myself. But half way back to the cottage I couldn't resist taking a peek inside the bag. At first I couldn't believe it; I checked again. It was there alright. Miss Heath had slipped in an extra boiled sweet! I even forgave her for calling them lollies.

November the 5th came and went, but there was no bonfire and no fireworks. I found solace in David Buck's new batch of comics, having once more regained favour with him. I would have liked to have thought that the old *Otranto* camaraderie had something to do with it, but I suspect that a sacrificial toffee had some influence in my reinstatement.

It didn't seem at all like Guy Fawkes weather. For a start there were no dead leaves like those of the English trees. And instead of the days getting shorter and colder, they were growing longer and warmer. Everything seemed back to front. In England, November would see the football season getting into its stride; out here, it had finished. Mr Barrett had already posted up the inter-cottage cricket fixtures, and with the lengthening days, it was growing light enough to get a bit of practice in between tea and bedtime.

Suddenly, after-school chores were being done in half the usual time. Those on wood-fetching consignments spent far less time in pinging at parrots with home-made 'gings' or exploring deep into the bush. Now it was very much a case of shouldering the first log you found and hurrying back with it to chop it up. Then there was little trouble in convincing Miss that we needed all the practice we could get. Rhodes seemed less fortunate than other cottages in the proportion of sportsmen it got when distribution of new arrivals were made; a fact that kept us well down the championship ladder.

With the cricket competition under way, Saturday afternoon on the sports ground was a mass of white-singleted boys. In addition to the centre wicket, six other pitches were spaced around the periphery of the ground. These were constructed from the loam of anthills, which, when watered and rolled, made an excellent surface. But with so many matches being played in such a confined area, there was always a danger of being hit with a ball from another game. It was not unknown for a batsman to be caught out by a player from a team two games away.

An Aussie Holiday

A month before Christmas all mail deliveries were suspended. The reason for this was to accumulate as much as possible for delivery on Christmas morning. The school broke up for the long summer holidays a few days before Christmas. During these long hot days with fierce sunsets it was difficult to work up any enthusiasm for the festive day. I would have been more at home doing my best to wear my boots out sliding the length of Eastcombe's frozen village green. However, by the time Christmas Eve came around, it was all hands on decorating the main dining hall and the cottages. Cottage Mothers helped children to hang the coloured paper chains from rafters and around the walls. Balloons and bells livened up the doorways; chimneys were swept, even though everyone knew that Father Christmas would arrive on the back of a truck with the mail.

Soon after sunrise on Christmas morning boys and girls set about their jobs with a rare vigour, eager to get them out of the way before breakfast. At eight o'clock a bugle call announced the arrival of Santa Claus in the village and discipline was suspended for the ecstatic moments when mailbags were opened and gifts disclosed. The same question was on everyone's lips: Will there be something for me? For most children there was. But some there were who had no relatives or friends to send them a Christmas message. With wistful eyes they watched the sorting of letters and parcels, not really expecting, but hoping for something — right until the last article had been taken from the bag. From deep within the mailbag I was handed a small parcel and letter from Mother, but I sadly missed the little stocking hanging from my bed.

But tears were soon wiped away. Gifts were waiting in Miss's room for those whom Santa had forgotten, and wistful eyes gleamed joyfully once more. For a while parcels were opened and letters were read. Then it was time to get ready for church.

Somehow the bell peeled with more animation, and children walked more briskly to church, their bare brown feet making whispers of sound as they moved into allotted pews. And soon the magnificent interior echoed to the chorus of clear young voices ringing with heart and soul, 'Christians awake, Salute the happy morn'.

To anyone listening to the service, it would have been difficult to imagine anyone being unhappy on this special day, my first Australian Christmas. Yet lying just beneath the surface of this facade of happiness there must have been many children who missed the company of former loved ones. Part of the joy of my earlier Christmases was the family closeness — the jaunt, almost, of clambering up the hill for the special service. Now, here in Australia, although the Cottage Mothers were pleasant enough on this special day, there remained a distinct feeling of remoteness between adult and child. For all the noble endeavour of institutions, one vital ingredient is always missing. There is, and never will be, a substitute for love.

With the service over, three hundred and fifty children trod the red dirt track under a blazing sun to the welcome shelter of the dining room. A battery of whirling ceiling fans rustled the branches of gum tips and flowers that decorated the tables and walls, and when we sat down to cold meat and salad my eyes misted in memory of a hot roast with all the trimmings, and pulling crackers with brother George while Father sharpened his carving knife on the steel before attacking the steaming turkey and Mother keeping an eye on the vegetables in the oven while stirring the gravy...

But there was plum pudding to follow, although it was boiled in the same cylindrical shaped steamed-plonk tins that were used during the year. Not that it made any difference really; when it was cut into fourteen slices and laced with custard it tasted equally as rich as the traditionally shaped Christmas puddings. And then we pushed the forms back to thank God for what we had received and returned to our cottages with our sweet and nut ration in our pocket to keep us going while we played with toys, buried our noses in David Buck's extra bundle of comics or simply re-read our letters. I read Mother's letter for the third time and inspected once more the beautiful blue tie she had sent me.

I made a promise then that even though I had to wear the official school tie at Fairbridge, on the day when I left I would wear her tie with my going away suit. But that day was nearly five years into the future. A lot was to happen before then.

The most immediate of these events happened the very next day. Half the kids from Fairbridge Farm invaded Mandurah. Boxing Day brought with it a flurry of preparation and excitement. There was so much to do that as soon as we showered, packing started. Bundles of blankets and clothes were tied and labelled, eating utensils and cutlery were crated and the last housework for seventeen days carried out. Then everything was stacked on the road verge awaiting the arrival of the truck. When it arrived there was a mad scramble of gear and bodies and a final wave to Miss as we left for our holiday.

Although Mandurah was only twenty-five kilometres away the drive took the best part of an hour. With the two trucks crammed to capacity with boisterous children the utmost care had to be taken. The last thing anyone wanted was an accident. For well over a decade the old faithful Reo truck had negotiated the journey dozens of times without mishap; now age had taken its toll of the engine, but the chassis lingered on as a horse-drawn wood cart. The replacement truck, together with Mr Nancarrow's Pinjarra-based carrier, now transported Fairbridgians to their idyllic holiday spot

Fairbridge Farm School's Reo truck.

on the coast.

Three kilometres of gravelled road took us out of Fairbridge property on to the main South-West Highway, and by the time we had reached the bitumen, the truck was rollicking with song. A succession of popular tunes of old England, Ireland, Scotland and Wales in keeping with the holiday spirit were reeled off one after the other with great gusto. We hadn't gone far before someone started up the school's favourite song in which the ancient Reo truck was sentimentally featured in doing what it did best — transporting Fairbridge kids to and from Mandurah. For well over a decade it had been handed down to new arrivals to keep the tradition going, and our lot had no intention of letting our forbears down. At a giddy twenty-five kilometres per hour we stormed into Pinjarra bawling our heads off for the benefit of our long-suffering friends in the town. The strong easterly wind carried the familiar Gundagai tune well in advance of our arrival, and as we grew nearer they caught the words:

There's a truck rattling back on the old Pinjarra track
Along the road to Fairbridge Farm,
For the radiator's hissing — the sparking plugs are
missing Beneath the summer sky,
For there's kero in the petrol and sand in the gears
And we haven't seen a garage for over forty years.
There's a Reo rattling back on the old Pinjarra track
Along the road to Fairbridge Farm.

And as we turned right into Pinjarra Road and headed for
Mandurah we were into our third chorus and just warming
up.

With the breeze behind us we fairly hurtled along the
flat coastal plain at fifty kilometres an hour, hanging grimly
on to our floppy sou'-wester hats. To lose one of these special
neck protectors was regarded as almost a crime. From the
start of summer the one protective measure that had been
drummed into us was the necessity to wear our hats against
the potential fatal effects of the fierce Australian sun.

But this slight inconvenience did nothing to dampen our
enthusiasm or lessen the sound of sheer exuberance as we
negotiated the bridges over the Murray and Serpentine rivers.
Then we were in Mandurah, but instead of going on over
the bridge that spanned the estuary, we turned right along
the foreshore skirting the waters of a shallow lagoon until
branching off on a track that took us around it, and stopped
at a clearing just before the Peninsular Hotel. A network
of marquees and tents told us that we had arrived.

After quickly unloading our camping gear from the truck
so that it could return to Fairbridge to fetch another load,
we moved it to our allotted tents. Lying alongside each tent
was a bundle of sacks and a few bales of straw. Then began
the novelty of stuffing straw into the bags to form a mattress
which, we were told, was known as a palliasse. I soon
discovered that although it filled to a great bulk to start
with, after a few days it had settled down to quite a thin
wafer.

By midday the camp had sorted itself out and when the
bugle sounded 'cookhouse' everyone made for the biggest

Mandurah foreshore. Footbridge in the background over the
Mandurah Lagoon to the Peninsular Hotel, c.1930.

marquee where we were told which seats to occupy. The
seats were made from bush saplings, an innovation I thought
that really added to the atmosphere of the camp. It certainly
didn't impair our appetites because dinner plates were
scraped in record time in anticipation of starting our holiday
in earnest. But before we could do this, Bonk had a few
words of wisdom for us.

He went on to say in an authoritative voice, that although
it was the intention of the staff to permit children to enjoy
themselves, it was imperative to maintain a high standard
of cleanliness in order to avoid any outbreak of illness which
would have inevitably spread quickly throughout the camp.
Therefore every effort had to be made to control the fly
problem and there was to be no slackening of discipline for
personal hygiene. To replace the customary morning shower,
it was to be compulsory for everyone to have a dip in the
lagoon. Fresh water had to be carted from a bore in

Fairbridge boys with the water cart at Mandurah, filling up from a bore near the town jetty. Hall's Head is in the background, early 1930's.

Mandurah, so special care had to be made to avoid wasting it.

The Colonel continued in a change of subject: 'At all times in your association with the local people, you will be judged by your behaviour. Remember, the good name of Fairbridge is your responsibility; do nothing to dishonour it. A programme of activity and competitions will be posted on the notice board daily, and you are encouraged to contribute to their success by active participation. I shall inspect the dining and living areas every morning at 9.00am sharp and a competition will be held, with a prize going to the cottage judged to have been the most efficient. At the completion of the inspection you will be free to enjoy yourselves.'

Mandurah in the '30s was a sleepy fishing resort consisting mainly of timber and fibro holiday cottages each with its own windmill-powered bore water supply or storage tanks that were filled from the run-off from the roofs. Two hotels and half a dozen shops were enough to meet the requirements of the town. One family of early settlers to the district, the Tuckey family, had built their home and shop on the prime waterfront site close to the bridge, while across the road Suttons occupied the tea-rooms on the strategic corner position. A few yards further along the waterfront was the well-named Renown Bakery whose produce enjoyed an excellent reputation far beyond the boundaries of the district. The other shops were dotted along the road. But perhaps the most popular establishment of all for us Fairbridge kids was the Capitol theatre. Apart from a very occasional showing of Hoot Gibson on the silent screen at the farm school, I hadn't seen a picture since my day out at Clapham.

But Mandurah's popularity stems from its waterways, the unique attraction being the Peel Inlet. This great expanse of water is almost a circular lake about sixteen kilometres across with an average depth of two metres and into which flows the Murray and Serpentine rivers. An extension of the inlet is the twenty-four-kilometres-long, three-kilometres-wide Harvey Estuary which is equally as shallow. In fact, some areas of both waterways are less than knee deep but the whole place is a prolific breeding ground for crabs, prawns and some species of fish. And there is a channel out to the Indian Ocean which gives vital access for the marine life, which in turn, guarantees a constant supply.

During my first year at Mandurah there were new and productive skills to learn: skills like trawling for prawns along the water's edge, and baiting a hook. And knowing what sized hook to use was important too. Some of the best fishing and prawning was to be had underneath the bridge. This was made possible by the thoughtful construction of a sizable fishing platform with a double access to the shore. So popular was this spot that some local authority had cut notches into the seating edges allotting each person an equal amount of room, and in certain times of the day or night, not only were people seated shoulder to shoulder, but there were others waiting behind them ready to occupy

Mouth of the estuary, Mandurah, c.1930.

immediately any abandoned position. And if you weren't lucky enough to get a spot, sometimes there was drama to watch, especially when the king prawns came floating through on an ebb tide.

To catch prawns in a scoop net it is necessary to have a very fine meshed net with a deep pocket, and, if you're operating from the bridge, you need a long handle. The fortunate ones are the people upstream in a boat. They get the first pickings with a short-handled net that is much easier to control. All they need is a bright gas lamp and a keen eye. Sometimes the prawns that get caught are the lucky ones; the survivors have only a brief respite.

Awaiting their passage under the bridge is a gallery of gas lamps and a battery of long-handled nets ready to pounce. As soon as a sighting is made, the action is on. There is no order given to commence battle — it would be extremely unwise to alert the opposition. It is then that the net with the longest handle comes into its own. A quick calculation is made. The range, which is diminishing with the approaching target, is being constantly judged. A muffled mutter alerts the unwatchful, an uncontrolled curse escapes selfish lips, nets are poised, breath is held ...

Suddenly, a salvo of shots strikes the water simultaneously. The silent river erupts into a boiling cauldron. Prawn vanishes and nets disappear beneath the brine from which they are hurriedly retrieved for inspection. But there is only one winner, and while he disentangles the prize, a second force of attackers waits in the rear in the hope of sighting another prawn while the others are still regrouping.

For hours the battle rages with little comment. There is a constant clash of armour, a choked oath, an occasional stifled cry. If a casualty withdraws, his place is immediately taken by a reservist, and the war continues unabated. Fortunately there are no serious injuries. But there are many observers.

The spectator seats are crowded with supporters watching with keen interest, slaking their thirst and appeasing their appetites from flasks and snack boxes. In addition, there is a continual stream of casual visitors taking a summer night's stroll, who peer inquisitively into half-filled buckets of water to observe the haul. With competition so keen there is little likelihood of a small Fairbridge lad getting a guernsey at the battle for the prawns. His chance is with the crabs.

To begin with, the tackle is more within his budget, particularly if two or three pool their resources. All that is required is a drop-net and a long length of rope. That gives an enterprising lad a start. By selling his catch for the day, he can add to his number of nets which hopefully increases his yield. The bait problem is usually solved by waiting for a fisherman to clean his catch, and latching on to the heads before the pelicans beat him to it. Very soon, if all goes well and the crabs are running, the young entrepreneur has enough capital to hire a boat and so he's on his way to making his first million.

But the sports-minded enthusiast who enjoys the thrill of the chase walks the shallows of the estuary with scoop

Fairbridge boys at Mandurah. The blond boy sitting in the boat is Tug Wilson.

net and tub, preferably when the water is calm so that the sighting of the prey is made easier and lessens the chance of placing an unprotected toe into the powerful claws of a big Blue Manna.

Fishing though, was the sport for everyone. With just ordinary hand-held green string or cat-gut lines, one or two hooks and a sinker, there was always a catch of sand-whiting to be made. And it didn't take long to learn the skills of the game; the tying on of a hook, when to use a running sinker, when not to use a sinker at all, and the subtleties of the different rigs. The greatest pleasure came when the catch was taken to the kitchen and the staff would cook it with all the others for a delicious meal of fresh fish.

And of course there was always the swimming. Mandurah's waterways catered for all tastes; from the sheltered, shallow lagoon to the deeper waters of the channel in which dolphins cruised leisurely between conveniently placed sand bars where the weaker swimmers could rest awhile before continuing on to reach their goal of the other

Swimming, Mandurah.

bank. But the most adventurous of all was the escape to the wilderness of Hall's Head where the giant rollers of the open sea swept in to pound on clean sandy beaches. Here we had our first thrill of trying to catch the great green curling waves that hurled us shorewards at a breathtaking pace to leave us panting at the water's edge and sometimes struggling to resist the drag of the receding foam.

A few minutes of this bruising treatment was all that the youngsters could take before retiring to join the horse that was resting in the shade of the shrub-covered sandhills. Old Dobin had just brought a tank full of water for us to slake our thirst before tackling the surf once more.

And while I rested, enjoying the spread of crashing seas beneath an expanse of deep blue sky, I couldn't help comparing it with the mud flats of Weston-Super-Mare. Although it lacked the sophistication, the amenities and the entertainment of its English counterpart, Mandurah in the '30s was an unspoilt paradise.

There were times though, when the Fairbridge children thought otherwise. Especially when we were all set to plunge into the lagoon immediately after reveille, only to find the tide was out and we had to run a couple of hundred metres to find water deep enough for our purposes. And even though it was summer, an early morning's easterly breeze whipping against wet bathers, could be quite a chilly experience.

We discovered too, that even in paradise, Bonk had no intention of lowering the standard of discipline. He had warned us about cleanliness and his first day's inspection was pitiless. Colonel Heath had not been a leader of men and the recipient of the Military Cross for nothing. He set the required standard from the outset and made sure that we understood. From then on the inter-cottage competition was conducted in earnest.

If a blanket was carelessly folded or out of alignment, it was a point docked. If the Colonel spotted a minute fragment of paper on the floor, it brought an immediate broadside: 'What's that newspaper doing on the ground?' he thundered. 'Don't you know that you must wait until after inspection before you bring out the morning paper? Hm — two marks.'

Similarly, his genius for exaggeration excelled in the mess hut; a crumb on the floor and he was away: 'What the devil are you throwing away that loaf of bread for?' he demanded. 'Don't you know that half the people of the world are starving?' And on it went. A fishbone became nothing smaller than a shark, and a small segment of wrapping paper that had escaped detection by fourteen pairs of eyes, but seen by Bonk, had him demanding why a pound of butter should be left lying on the ground. 'Three marks!' echoed the dismal tidings, as his assistant reached for the pencil.

With the inspection over, the rest of the day was ours. The duty mess orderlies had a little extra to do before and after meals, but it was done quickly enough and little free time was lost. In the first day or two, it was only natural that everyone wanted to slip into town to see what the shops had to offer and to sample the luxury of an ice-cream.

There were two ways to reach the town from the camp on the peninsular. You could follow the road around the lagoon, or take the short cut to the foreshore across the

Fairbridge girls in front of one of the tents at Mandurah.

rickety old footbridge. However, that way was fraught with danger. The ageing bridge planks may once have been flush fitting and close, but years of weathering in a hostile environment had shrunk the boards into little more than slats. But unfortunately the shrinking had not been uniform, so that some slats protruded up to an inch above the others. In addition, the nails had become so corroded over the years that most of the slats had worked loose. For barefooted children it came a challenge to complete the crossing unscathed. And this was very rarely accomplished, even during daylight hours and using exaggerated high steps; imagine the difficulty a night crossing caused.

A night crossing returning after the pictures became almost obligatory unless you walked four times the distance around the road. This might have suited the bigger boys when dawdling their girl friends home from the pictures, but most of us preferred to take the risk of a stubbed toe or a splintered foot across the bridge. Only very occasionally did someone twist an ankle or miss a handrail and finish up in the drink.

The pictures, of course, were never missed, unless you ran out of money. An open-air theatre was something to write home about, especially for us English kids. Everything was out in the open including the big screen. And in the fence a gate at the side of the screen opened onto a sloped area that was three parts filled with deck chairs. It was like sitting on a sandless beach at night. England was nothing like this.

Apart from the fishing, the cinema was the night life of the town. And after a year-long bedtime of eight o'clock, not one of us intentionally missed out on a chance to stay out late.

The proprietors of the Capitol theatre made special concessions for Fairbridge children. For threepence, we could sit on the grassed area between the deck chairs and the screen, and although this meant watching a distorted picture with stretched necks, it was not enough to deter the enthusiasm or lessen the enjoyment of the show. In any event this small inconvenience was resolved when the picture started, by the older children occupying the empty chairs, which in turn gave the others a chance to move back. For days after a picture night we relived the most exciting episodes time and time again, extracting the very last scrap of value for our threepence. The highlight of our holiday was the free picture night especially appreciated by the many who had run out of funds. As the occasion usually celebrated the end of the camp, those who had money left let their heads go in a final orgy of spending. Even some of the paupers might be permitted a lick or two of an ice-cream.

The day before we packed up was a busy one. With Bonk going the rounds on his last inspection, conjecture was keen on who would take out the Most Efficient Cottage prize. And always, he saw to it that the finish was close; there was nothing like competition to stimulate and maintain a healthy interest in things. The place-getters were announced at dinner time amid a mixture of enthusiastic applause and a lot of good-natured banter. Whatever the prize, it usually came out of the Colonel's pocket and just in time for it to be spent.

But all too soon the morning arrived when we had to pack up for the return to Fairbridge. Understandably, this was done with a lot less enthusiasm than before, but we all had many happy memories to sustain us for another year. And no matter how deflated we felt, nothing could stop us putting all we had into the singing of the Fairbridge song, the most raucous chorus of which we reserved for the Pinjarra people.

With the dumping of our gear outside the cottages it was back to work. Blankets were trodden on in the bath to remove the salt, shorts and shirts were washed on the old scrubbing board, and cutlery resuscitated with a liberal application of Bon-ami. Miss greeted us with the news that a new work roster was on the notice board.

Our Mandurah holiday included only half the school; the other half went in the trucks that brought us back. Having had a period of unrestricted opportunity for swimming, we were anxious to keep it going in the river for as long as the school holidays lasted. But the river had not yet been

153

At the swimming hole, Frances Trussler and Jane Paterson
in the foreground.

dammed, which created a few problems during that first summer.

Summers in this part of the world are long hot and dry, with very little rain falling for four or five months, during which the South Dandalup River dries up considerably to expose a river bed littered with the debris of fallen tree trunks and roots. Only a handful of water holes suitable for swimming existed and these were formed by an odd tree falling in the right place.

The other problem lay in the fact that we now required the supervision of a Cottage Mother when we went swimming. This in turn put the pressure on us boys not to do anything that would antagonise Miss. It was all too easy for her to withhold the privilege, a fact that became the Cottage Mother's most effective disciplinary weapon. But in all fairness the walk to and from the swimming holes would have taxed the strength of the more elderly of the Cottage Mothers, particularly on a very hot day. Although Miss Wellard and Miss Fraser weren't exactly young, they took their children swimming practically every day. In fact, Nelson cottage had such a stalwart in Miss Wellard that during the cricket season she undertook the self-appointed task of scorer, with the result that her boys rarely lost a match.

Nelson was just over the road from Rhodes, and on many evenings I watched enviously as they made their way to the river with Miss Wellard's chair carried high on the head of one of her boys. Nelson may not have been one of the fashionable cottages, but their Cottage Mother was a woman whose sole purpose was the welfare of her boys.

Rhodes's choice of pools led past the Founder's grave and along a path that wound down to the river. Along the way, Miss instructed me to walk before her to hold back the foliage that spread across the track. 'One day Ramsbottom', she said, 'this is the sort of behaviour I'd expect you to do for your young lady, especially when you are out courting'. Although I was happy enough to help Miss in this way, her words seemed to me to be a futile wish. At that time I couldn't possibly imagine any girl wanting to share my name.

As we neared the valley, a murmur of water drifted through the evening heat, setting a gentle rhythm to the performance of the hidden birds as they thrilled and chuckled from the safety of bulky red gums and slim saplings. With the invasion of their territory, this pleasant harmony would soon be overpowered by the raucous enthusiasm of liberated children at play.

For an hour we splashed and played in the muddy water pausing only to tear off a leach. We non-swimmers kept to the shallows while the others dived or jumped into the deep water from the trunk and roots of trees that formed the pool. When Miss called us out, the older boys saw to it that the young ones acted promptly; they had no intention of letting anyone jeopardise future swimming jaunts. After I towelled myself down, I recovered my walking stick, and dutifully took up my position as Miss's protector for the return walk.

Occasionally Miss took us into the hills. Here was new adventure scrambling over rocks, down gullies and climbing the steep rise to stand on the huge granite boulder from where the wide expanse of the coastal plane could be viewed, and kangaroos could be seen grazing in the scattered patches of grass. But the hills were popular for the waterfalls that cascaded over the boulder-strewn water course. The favourite spot was a deep natural hole fed by a slide, smoothed over the centuries into an idyllic water playground. Here was an environment far different from the smoggy streets of London; here was freedom and laughter and fun.

In less than a year, I had escaped from the gloom of London to the beauty of the bush under the tall ceiling of blue Australian skies. A pattern of life was emerging. The strict disciplined routine of institutional life was relieved at regular intervals by periods of comparative freedom, but always under supervision wherever potential danger lurked, enough to give a sense of security. It would not — could not — ever compensate for the loss of parental love and the life in my Cotswold village, but as a substitute, it was a compromise of experiences to which I managed to make a healthy adjustment.

NEW CHUMS NO MORE

When school resumed, I went into Miss Young's class. She was a slim, athletic person with nearly always a smile on her lean face. From the very first day I made up my mind to do well in her class.

In the meantime, another party of children had arrived which meant that the *Otranto* party was no longer the 'new chums'. This gave us a feeling of maturity, a certain status. We qualified now to give advice. The little tricks of the trade were being learnt that made life a little less traumatic; dodges like holding a broom under the spray from the shower, although this was fraught with danger if a 'tattle-tale' saw it and whined about it. It was a definite advantage to remain popular with the other boys. For me, this was not always easy.

With the cottage cleaning roster changing regularly, it was only a matter of time before I graduated through all the jobs that guaranteed cleanliness of cottage and clothes. In a comparatively short time I could set tables, wash dishes, wash shirts and pants on a corrugated scrubbing board, scrub floors and polish jarrah floor boards.

The two cleaning agencies were kerosene and phenyl, and Miss took great care to see that they were used to advantage. I never realised just how complicated scrubbing a floor could be. Everything had to be done to a routine, the basic requirements being a bucket of water spiked with phenyl, a floor cloth, a scrubbing brush and a slab of washing soap. Then, with me on my knees and Miss standing over me, the instruction began.

'Start from a corner and use the cloth to wet a patch of floor.' From then on the orders came thick and fast. 'Don't try to do too much at a time ... Put a little more water on the floor ... only half wring out the cloth ... no, that's not the way to wring out a cloth. I'll show you once, and remember, there's only one correct way to do anything. Now, watch and listen ...'

I resumed my efforts, but with so many instructions I was becoming confused. And still the lesson continued.

'Right ... that's enough. Now wipe up the dirty suds with the cloth ... you will find you will have to wring the cloth out two or three times before the floor is dry enough.'

It took five minutes to do just one small patch. There was the whole floor to do. I was almost in tears thinking I'd never get through it all in time for school. But there was still more to come.

'Now, do the floor along the wall. Always remember this Ramsbottom, if you do the corners and sides first, the middle will do itself.'

That was her parting gem. To this day I have not forgotten how to scrub a floor. Only these days I don't get down on my hands and knees.

The polished boards of the living room and the dormitory received an application of kerosene on Saturday mornings, after which they were polished. Every other day they were swept and polished only. Because of its size, the dormitory became very irksome working on hands and knees, so the engineers among us came up with a device to lighten the work load.

A large wooden block bound with layers of cloth and fitted to a long handle revolutionised the cleaning. Another dimension was added when it was discovered that by reinforcing the joint between block and handle it became strong enough to hold a boy's weight. So with the beds pushed to one end, a miniature drag strip resulted, with pusher and passenger taking turns. There were minor breakdowns of course, but these were rectified by the trial and error method.

Cleaning the dormitory very soon became the most popular job, but looking after the Cottage Mother came a close second. Mrs Tomkinson's floor was covered by a carpet square so all her room required was a sweep and dusting. True, there was her breakfast to fetch from the servery, but that was little enough. It was in the evening that Miss's job turned out interesting.

She received ingredients for her evening meal from the store; things like butter, eggs and tea. In addition, she sometimes preferred not to eat a cooked breakfast, but took her uncooked rations back to the cottage to augment the other supplies. To keep these perishables fresh every cottage had a cooling system generally known as a Coolgardie Safe.

This contraption consisted of a hessian-covered metal frame about fifty centimetres square and one metre tall, with a hinged door giving access to three compartments separated by tin shelving. The top of the frame became a reservoir by extending the sides ten centimetres above the roof. This held several gallons of water into which strips of cloth hung from all sides over the edge and down the outside. Once these were saturated, water slowly permeated down the walls of the safe into a tray with a built-in outlet. The whole structure stood on a strong metal-framed base about thirty centimetres off the floor. By keeping the safe on a shaded verandah, and allowing the wind to blow freely around the moist sides, it was surprising how cool the interior became. Naturally, its efficiency depended on the reservoir being topped up, which became the responsibility of Miss's boy.

When my turn came round for this job, I tried always to watch her cook her evening meal, particularly omelettes, which seemed to be one of her favourite meals. After a couple of weeks of observing and asking questions, I asked Miss if I could have a go at making one for her. She not only agreed, but stayed with me to supervise my efforts, with the result that between us we cooked a very satisfactory meal. At least, I thoroughly enjoyed the generous portion that she gave me. That was one of the perks of the job; you not only got Miss's leftovers, but you also got to lick her cooking utensils clean. But perhaps the best perk of all was in making her a cup of tea; you always managed to squeeze a cup out for yourself sweetened, naturally enough, with a couple of teaspoons of her sugar. It made a welcome change from the eternal cocoa.

Of the many after-school chores, fetching the daily milk ration was probably the easiest. The distribution centre was outside the rear door of the main dining hall, where a billy can from each cottage was placed on a table abutting the building. When the milk cart arrived from the dairy, the main kitchen's requirements were met first and the remainder was divided among the cottages. The senior Cottage Mother, Mrs Huxham, dished it out with the aid of one and two-pint ladles. She was a quaintly old-fashioned woman with a penchant for wearing black, and was not one to suffer fools gladly. Her tongue matched her features, and woe betide any child who arrived late on the scene.

My favourite after-school chore was the walk into the bush for a log of wood, or a sugar bag load of gravel. To me it was an hour of freedom. Although we had no watches, experience gave us our own sense of timing. I learnt to read the sun and the shadows, but when these were hidden, mistakes could prove costly. A return to the cottage too early and another job could be found; too late, and the penalty could be a cold bath in the residual water of a dozen dirty boys, plus an extra load of gravel the following night for loitering. So the punishment became an incentive to learn all the quicker.

But the environment of the bush was nearly every small boy's dream. To me, it was an education, a time of discovery. I learnt to identify the gum trees, the banksias, the sheoaks and the paper barks. In September the bush became a mass of colour with the wattles, the lescenaultia, hovea, and the distinctive red and green kangaroo paws. More importantly, I was fast becoming a seasoned veteran; I could run through the scrub and along the cruellest of gravel paths with the best of them now. I was fast becoming a little Aussie.

Carting firewood.

At the 1934 school sports meeting, I was successful in winning the medal for the Junior Champion Athlete although I was hard-pressed by the improving Jock Paterson. But another opportunity came my way when Miss Young chose me to play the part of Tom Sawyer in the school's end of year concert. She had introduced the book to us through the year, so the story was quite familiar, but in choosing me to play Tom, she unleashed a barrage of accusation that I was teacher's pet. But I found little trouble in coping with that; it was nothing in comparison to what I had been used to.

With a girl from the *Otranto* party as my Aunt Polly, and a dark-haired lad named Ken Dearlove as Huckleberry Finn, rehearsals started in the classroom. As the concert time drew near and the cast became more confident under Miss Young's direction, the classroom rocked under the enthusiasm of some pretty realistic acting.

The fight scene between the 'new boy' and Tom had Stuart Macklin and myself rolling around the floor until his cries of anguish brought Mr Healey charging across from three

161

classrooms away to find out the cause of the disturbance. But when it came to the actual performance it was Kenny Dearlove who got all the accolade — he and his dead cat.

It was in 1934 also, that the Fairbridge Farm Brass Band was formed. An item in the weekly routine orders invited any boy who was interested to report to Mr Shugar in the main dining hall on the following Sunday afternoon. Mr Shugar was the cook at the farm school, but before he and his wife came from England, he had spent several years in the Scots Guards Band. Now, mainly through the fund-raising efforts of the sports mistress, Mrs Groom, Fairbridge had its own brass instruments.

On that first audition it was surprising just how many boys failed the simple aural test that Mr Shugar put us through. I hadn't had any previous musical knowledge, but like so many other children, thought that the band would be some sort of glamorous job. Right from the start we found that it was going to be a lot of hard work. Those that failed to sing or whistle in tune were discarded; the thirty of us who were left, went back to our cottage smug in the belief that we would be playing tunes in a month.

What a shock it was to be told then that it would be six months before we would be allowed to touch an instrument. At our first get-together, instead of music stands and noise, there were blackboards and chalk. A whole new language had to be learnt; a language of signs and symbols. For two evenings a week after school, the band battled it out, and during the six months' 'donkey work' as Mr Shugar called it, only four or five gave it away.

Eventually graduation night came around; the night when instruments were to be handed out. Excitement was rife as twenty-four boys were presented with cornets, tenor horns, baritones, euphoniums, trombones and basses. The side and bass drums would come later. No Buckingham Palace investiture could have been more meaningful; no prize more treasured.

It was purely Mr Shugar's experience that dictated the distribution of instruments; thin-lipped boys were given cornets, with the larger mouth-pieced instruments going to the full-lipped. I was given a trombone.

If we thought the months of theory were a long hard grind, we weren't prepared for the shocking array of noises that gurgled and farted from somewhere out of the maze of tubing at the first attempt to produce a note. It would have been understandable if Mr Shugar had packed it in right there and then. But, being the experienced musician that he was, he set out on his mammoth task with methodical efficiency.

Each instrumental group reported to him in turn immediately after school, and the first lesson was the care and maintenance of instruments. He explained the reason for such highly skilled engineering behind the manufacture of each instrument; the need for care in handling it especially when it was not played. He emphasized the need for cleanliness; to wash it through with hot, soapy water, with special attention given to the mouthpiece. And finally he stressed the importance of appearance, particularly when the band became available for engagements. Harry Butler and David Foulkes were my fellow trombonists. Our tuition day was on every Tuesday and we came in for special attention.

'Because of the trombone's straight tubing, you boys need to be extra careful in the handling of it. One small dent in the slide can do irreparable damage. You have the responsibility for its safety at all times.' That was Mr Shugar's way. No beating about the bush; no room for ambiguity. Ours was the pride of ownership.

For the first few weeks there were some weird sounds to be heard coming from the main kitchen after four o'clock. Very often emotions ran high; frustrations built up, simmered for a time, then spilled into tears. Yet through it all, Mr Shugar coaxed, encouraged, pleaded and sometimes demanded that we try harder, concentrate more, talk less and listen longer. He grew to know the temperament of each boy, how much each individual could take. And gradually his patience and understanding was rewarded with progress. Sounds became notes, and notes began to sound tuneful. Soon scales were being mastered. The band was taking shape.

Full band practice was held every Wednesday and Friday

Mr. Shugar conducting the Fairbridge Band outside the dining hall. Jack Ramsbottom is playing the trombone on the extreme left, c.1935.

night and anyone not attending needed a very good excuse. Colonel Heath, being the old soldier that he was, had the band's interest at heart, and let nothing impede its progress. Cottage Mothers were instructed to free their band boys from all other chores in order to attend band practice and Mr Shugar himself had threatened any truant with instant dismissal. He wasn't going to have anyone waste his and everyone else's time.

He and his wife were employed at Fairbridge as cooks, for which they received a modest wage out of which they had to pay rent for their small cottage behind the cookhouse. Mr Shugar received no extra payment for his time, effort and expertise in forming and training the band. In fact it cost him money.

Every Friday night, with instruments back in their cases and stored away after band rehearsal, he would produce a paper bag full of penny chocolate frogs and ceremoniously give one to each of us together with a good-natured quip

Fairbridge Farm School Band, Jack Ramsbottom, front row, centre.

or word of advice. But, on this occasion, never a criticism. This was a ritual to be savoured. We loved him for it.

Nineteen thirty-five was a year to be remembered. In November I became a teenager, it was also the Silver Jubilee of the reign of King George V, and to celebrate the occasion every Fairbridge child was presented with a medallion.

During the year, one of the King's sons, the Duke of Gloucester visited Australia and his itinerary included a short visit to Fairbridge. Bonk saw it as an ideal opportunity for the band to make its debut, despite Mr Shugar's protests that it was not yet ready. But the Colonel insisted that the band play the National Anthem at the official welcome outside the church.

And despite our unpreparedness, the band was lined up on parade, music in card holders and the order for the Royal Salute given. The National Anthem was played, but the arrangement was unique. Mr Shugar had solved the problem by giving everyone the melody to play with the fingering or slide positions written in beneath each note. The band had arrived.

The day following the Duke's visit was a day almost too thrilling to be real. The magnificent Grenadier Guards Band called in to see us. In reality, its musical director, Major Miller brought his band from Perth as a compliment to Colonel Heath who was a former Guardsman. But the whole school shared in the Colonel's pleasure as the band marched and counter-marched up and down the hockey field behind the church.

The mood changed when the moustached Director with a double row of military ribbons adorning the left breast of his long frock coat took over from the giant Drum-Major. In his braided peaked cap, immaculate white gloves and with ceremonial sword at the hip, he wielded the baton with authoritative flourish. The pageant of marching had been stirring enough: now the band played tingling arrangements of traditional melodies culminating in a moving rendition of *Roses of Picardy*. For the members of the Fairbridge fledgling band, and for me in particular, listening to the music of such a famous British Military Band that seemingly had marched into our lives straight out of the pages of history, was an experience beyond measure. When I stood on the dirt road and waved their coach good-bye, I had an unexplainable feeling of sadness, an emptiness, as though I had lost something precious.

When reality returned, and I recalled that the sum total of my musical ability was a couple of fuzzy-sounding scales, I realised that I had a long way to go in the music business. But the visit of the Grenadier Guards Band must have subconsciously inspired our small group of battlers, because from that moment on, our band improved rapidly. Within a few weeks we were playing simple tunes from our tutors, and from there, we tackled our first march. It is a tune I shall never forget; it is called *When Jesus Comes*. We played no other march for twelve months.

But it was one thing to play sitting down, and something quite different to play on the march. During the long summer evenings the sound of our one march drifted back on the

Major Miller, Director of Music, Grenadier Guards Band, with Fairbridge girl, 1935.

The Grenadier Guards Band playing at Fairbridge. The church is in the background, 1935.

sea breeze as we trod the track on the road to perfection.

Eventually the time came when Mr Shugar considered that the band was ready for its first public appearance. And it was an occasion not to be taken lightly. Colonel Heath was invited to the final rehearsal to give official approval and consent for the inaugural event.

The announcement was made at breakfast time the following morning. Despite the persistent rumours that spread throughout the village, the dining hall came to a hushed standstill as Bonk strode purposefully to his customary position and in his familiar military stand-at-ease pose, with empty left sleeve tucked into his coat pocket, began:

'I have an historic announcement to make. The School Band will play a programme of light music outside this hall immediately after next Sunday's church service. Cottage Mothers will see that everyone who is not engaged in mess duties will attend.'

That was it. The Colonel had issued the order, and the

band had been guaranteed its first audience. But, captive audience though it may have been, we were given generous applause after each short melody. We methodically worked through our tutors which were held in our card holders as we stood for the performance. But even this slight inconvenience passed unnoticed as we warmed to the reception given to us. And after each item, a suited Mr Shugar turned to his audience to give a slight nod and a wide smile of acknowledgement. And well he might have been pleased; a year's hard persistence had come to fruition. No prouder man ever held a baton.

From that day on, the band went from strength to strength. More music was bought, our repertoire grew, our reputation spread. Requests for our services came in from surrounding organizations and individuals. We performed at the inter-school sports meeting, at various flower shows and on the Mandurah foreshore. With the approach of Christmas the band was in greater demand than ever. We even played carols outside Pinjarra's Premier Hotel with the publican keeping us well topped up with lemonade. Naturally, with perks like that, we kids didn't mind how many engagements we played at. It did wonders for our egos. When children of Australian families gathered around our music stands to listen to the achievements of orphaned Fairbridge kids, it gave me personally a warm feeling of self-esteem; a realisation that, after all, we were not so underprivileged, we were worth something to the community.

Meanwhile back at Fairbridge, the band added atmosphere and tradition to our own Christmas season by playing carols beneath the dim street lights that were scattered throughout the village. For the first time since my carol singing nights around Bismore and Eastcombe, I felt some familiarity with the festive season.

But the achievements of the school band were not the only thing of note to happen to Fairbridge throughout that long hard year of endeavour. As part of the nation's Silver Jubilee celebrations, the whole school was taken to Perth for a day out.

It was unbelievable. Nothing on such a grand scale had

ever happened before. It was a thrill even to walk into Pinjarra to catch the special train. It was a small price to pay for the privilege of seeing the city dressed up and illuminated in honour of the occasion. The train trip alone would have been enough to have made our day, but add a picture show and a trip on a ferry to the zoo, and it was more than we had dared hope for. But still there was more. A meal in the Town Hall put us all in good spirits to gaze in wonder at the fabulous neon lights and floodlit buildings that transformed Perth into a picture wonderland. Although it was very late by the time we got to bed that night, we all agreed that it had been a special day to remember.

UNPALATABLE RICE AND FRESH APRICOTS

One day Mrs Tomkinson called us together to tell us that Colonel Heath thought that she was getting too old to look after fourteen children, so she was being retired.

I was genuinely sorry to see her go, although her departure conformed to a pattern of semi-permanency with all my maternal relationships. Although there was no comparison between her and my mother, she had been a woman of compassion who had invited us on many a cold winter's evening to sit on her carpet in front of a homely fire and share her newspaper. She had done her job well. She had corrected our mistakes, taught us new skills (humble though they were), advised us on simple etiquette, and had appointed me sports captain of Rhodes.

The only altercation I had had with her in the two years since my arrival had been through a mistake. It happened one evening while reading the paper in her room when I was surprised to see an item of special interest and couldn't help reading it out. 'Bradman has had an operation for appendicitis while the rest of the Australian cricketers are on the way home by sea.' No sooner had the last word been spoken, when Miss rocked me with a slap around the face.

'How dare you say that!' she cried angrily.

'But it's here in the paper Miss, see — "Bradman has Operation".'

'Did you say Bradman?'

'Yes Miss, here is the heading.' I pointed to the paragraph, my ear still ringing. The fact was that one of our boys, Walter Bedwell, had been taken to hospital that very day with severe abdominal pains. She obviously had heard the name wrong.

'Well, in that case, I'm very sorry', she said apologetically. The peculiar outcome of that unfortunate episode, was that the very next day, Bedwell did have an appendectomy.

Another more personal setback happened to me at about this time. I was losing weight. Sister Bargh discovered it doing her regular check-up, with the result that I was put on a special diet. Despite the weight loss, I hadn't felt ill at all, and to suddenly find myself with a weekly ration of six eggs and half a pound of butter, felt like I was in a permanent party. Unfortunately the party lasted only three months, by which time it was decided that I was out of danger and fit enough to go back onto bread and dripping.

Our new Cottage Mother was Miss Rice. A tallish woman in her late thirties, with shrewd face and just a trace of red in her dark brown hair, she settled straight into a no-nonsense routine. Her thin lips emphasised a firmness of purpose that was substantiated by her actions. She was also unmarried.

She established her authority from the start by supervising our morning shower. At twelve years of age it made me feel uncomfortable, and there were older boys than I, but there was no understanding their feelings. And even though she ordered us to turn our backs, there was still something uncommonly curious about it.

When the weather warmed up and the risk of dodging the morning shower lessened, she introduced a game of forfeits. A minimum of ten minutes was allowed, timed from the last note of reveille, to make our bed and have a shower and report to her bedside which was now on her front verandah. She preferred to sleep there during the summer.

This was no problem for most of us, but the same couldn't be said for the smaller ones. Unfortunately for them, Miss was obviously not familiar with the system of handicapping that gives, or at least, tries to give all starters an equal chance. She made the rules, and that was that. There was no higher authority to whom an appeal could be made, although I suppose that some enterprising older boy could have asked to have been fronted up before Bonk. But it was never thought of. I suppose the system could be labelled as 'institutional democracy'. It wouldn't have been quite so bad even with the anomaly, if the penalty for a late finish had been some extra duty, but when the punishment was a deprivation of food, the fairness of the game must be questioned.

When breakfast constitutes a plate of porridge and some dripping and jam on dry bread, the withholding of the jam takes away the one ingredient that makes the meal palatable. Little David Buck, the baby of the cottage, had more than his share of unpalatable breakfasts. His was a good week if he'd had jam three times.

David came in for some more attention shortly after. Because he was so young, Miss Rice installed him as the permanent lavatory cleaner. It was a simple task of sweeping it out, washing the seat and floor, and keeping up the supply of newspaper squares that hung on the wall.

The problem was, of course, that the work could only be done while the premises were vacant, and with fourteen boys clamouring for patronage first thing in the morning, there was not a lot of time left for David to complete the job. Not that it worried David. Of all the boys in the cottage, he was the most even tempered and gentlest mannered. He was not one to let a small problem of time upset him. He had his own unique method of dealing with the situation; a situation in which he introduced the normal healthy boy's capacity for improvisation. When the lavatory was occupied, he didn't just wait around wasting the morning.

He used his imagination. To David, it became a number of things. One day it was a sentry box, another a palace. But whatever structure it assumed, he was the sole custodian, and as such, he had the responsibility of defending it at all costs and with every means at his disposal.

Once again this was not a problem for David. In the worn out straw broom he used for cleaning, he had a ready-made latest fashioned rifle, which meant he was now a soldier.

And in the tradition of all good soldiers, his drill had to be 'spot on'. He had seen that for himself on the *Otranto*. He had watched the British soldiers drilling, drilling, drilling. So each morning, with the Palace in residency, David marched up and down with rifle at the slope guarding his place with military precision. So that was the situation: day after day, a small boy with initiative and imagination turning a menial task into an interesting and harmless game.

Until one morning, when Miss blundered right into the sentry's path. That was the end of David Buck's phantom military career. Miss could hardly contain herself until she returned inside to gloat over her discovery. If she thought that she would get a response from the rest of us, she was doomed to disappointment. We were well aware of David's self-appointed position, and in fact, sometimes went along with him by asking permission for admittance. But for all his innovation, from that day on, Miss labelled him with the insensitive and unkind tag of 'unconscious'.

With over three hundred children living in one community, it was only natural that friction flared from time to time and in Rhodes cottage there was no exception to this. If anything, the unpleasantries had grown worse since the arrival of Miss Rice with her unpredictable style of discipline. Just when everything seemed to be going along smoothly, she would blow some minor incident up out of all proportion, and chaos would result. Not that we children were entirely blameless; we weren't, and no doubt our behaviour at times could be extremely trying, but there were occasions when the punishment was excessive.

An example of this treatment was given to me after a series of niggling behaviour between two of us. It was the usual irritating confrontation of me giving the other chap a nudge or a push and him retaliating with a whinge and a whine. Then it deteriorated into a verbal battle loud enough for Miss to hear: 'Miss, Ramsbottom's pushing me', or 'Ramsbottom hit me Miss (whine ... whine).'

And Miss couldn't fail to hear the little twerp because in the next breath, without so much as a request for an explanation, she let fly with an order: 'Ramsbottom, you will scrub the bathroom floor immediately.' Fuming with indignation at the injustice of being punished without a trial, I splashed and banged my way around troughs and bath taking my anger out on the floor with scrubbing brush and soap. Never had the bathroom floor been scrubbed so thoroughly. I was just starting to recover by the time I reported to Miss that I had finished it, when, without a moment's hesitation she replied, 'For being so smart, you can do it over again — quieter'.

The bitterness welled in my throat, almost choking me. I felt utter frustration and helplessness, dispirited, beaten. But there was no fighting it. Any rebellion and it was up before the Principal. The sheer weight of authority was too formidable an obstacle, too high a hurdle to tackle. Too many trips to the Principal's office and a personal file was in danger of becoming unhealthy, and eventually obese. And above all, there was the ultimate threat of being sent back to England in disgrace as unsuitable. A failure.

So in my experience there was no relief from the tension of injustice, no opportunity for counselling, and no sympathy. Only a crushing bitter feeling of defeat. For all I know, that method of punishment proved to be a success because, from then on, I became more selective in the choice of location where I could correct the little groveller's unfortunate habit.

There was no doubt that successive Fairbridge Society committees in Perth made every effort to preserve and develop the Founder's dream of a better life in Australia for underprivileged British children. Despite the fact that so much of the day was, of necessity, spent in maintaining the cleanliness of the cottages and doing general duties, a comprehensive range of sporting and recreational activities was made available to us. For example, both boys and girls were taught tennis under the guidance of a kindly white-haired sports mistress named Mrs Groom. Her enthusiasm kept three grass and three hard courts going in continuous use in order to give as many children as possible an opportunity to learn the game.

Another favourite pastime featuring boys and girls was the introduction of old-time dancing lessons during the winter months. Here the dapper Mr Barrett was in his element. Prancing about in his light plimsolls, he demonstrated the steps to the Gypsy Tap, the Military Two-step, the Gay Gordons and the Canadian Barn Dance. These were the evenings when the dining hall filled with the muffled shuffles of dozens of barefooted children in their progress around the hall. There were moments too when budding romances momentarily bloomed when boy asked girl to dance. But there was little chance of anything other than the most innocent of flirtations.

The flirtation barn dance presented the best opportunity for this. It was a case of making the most of an opportunity whenever the girl of your fancy came around. There was always the risk of a humiliating rejection, but that chance just had to be taken. Sometimes a doubtful position could be clarified when the understanding Mr Barrett came to the rescue by announcing 'ladies' choice'. Not that the choice did anything for me; my heart's desire usually chose some other dill. But naturally, attachments were made and romances did develop; nothing too serious, but enough for all the school to discover which boy was on with which girl. And gossip spread fast when affections cooled and alliances changed. Even though dancing may not have been a strong point, the lessons were nights not to be missed for their social value alone.

When the dancing lessons were over, Mr Barrett's experience of life was demonstrated again by keeping the boys back fifteen minutes after the girls were let out. Still there were always a few girls and boys who were motivated enough to send written messages, usually passed on by a sympathetic intermediary; and although risky, it usually came off. But the law of averages caught up with one lad when a 'love note' was intercepted by a Cottage Mother who gave it to the Principal of the time. The note was signed.

At dinner time the next day the boy was made to stand out in front of the whole school while his letter was read. In my mind, there could be nothing more cruel than to be publicly exposed to the ridicule to which this boy was being subjected. The reading was frequently interrupted by howls of laughter as mindless children were manipulated into reducing one of their own to a pitiful wreck. No doubt the boy had his sympathisers, but they were outnumbered. It was unfortunate that in an institution where so much time and effort had been spent to lessen the suffering of so called underprivileged children, such archaic treatment still existed.

In 1936 I joined the scouts. Several of my best friends were already in the movement, and although the band took up a lot of my time, I was keen to follow them. Besides, the happy memories of cub days which had made Clapham life more interesting helped to reinforce my decision.

And right from the time I was welcomed by Mr Branson, our scoutmaster, I knew I was going to like it. A man in his thirties, Mr Branson couldn't have been a better choice. He was a big athletic type of man with handsome features enhanced by a spruce moustache, and he had the knack of putting you immediately at ease by his relaxed manner.

The dozen or so of us quickly established a pleasant atmosphere in which we learnt new scouting skills and games. In a sense we became an elite little group, moreover the responsibility tag that came with being a scout, brought certain privileges that were not possible to grant to the rest of the school. For instance, one of the Pinjarra Patersons permitted us to camp for a few days on his riverside property.

It was an exhilarating experience; camped beside a water hole on the Murray River, making our own decisions, deciding what to cook from the rations that had been provided. This was what scouting was all about; adventure, decisions, comradeship, survival. We returned to Fairbridge in the school's utility with a satisfying sense of appreciation and accomplishment, and above all, a taste of approaching adulthood.

Our skills were given another opportunity to develop during the Mandurah camp a year later. By this time Fairbridge had lost its Peninsular site and had established itself at a perfect position across the water on the Halls Head side of the inlet. Land had been bought, huts had been

Fairbridge Scout Troop. Jack Ramsbottom at centre in a suit. Back row, left, Dick Darrington; front row, centre, Stan Trigg.

erected; we now had a permanent holiday home.

Stan Trigg, Dick Darrington and myself teamed up for a survival test. Mr Branson had arranged for us to camp overnight at the estuary house of an old Mandurah fisherman, Mr Cox. In the morning he would direct us towards the ocean and we would follow the coastline back to Halls Head. A faint track, barely visible through the thick scrub, would lead to Mr Cox's place eight kilometres away.

With nothing but rations in our haversacks the three of us set off in good humour; found the track through the shady bush, and enjoyed the two-hour hike to the cottage where Mr Cox welcomed us. If we hadn't known his occupation before we saw him, we would have known immediately on arrival. A short distance from the stone cottage on the edge of the shallow water, several folds of fishing net hung from bush-timbered frames while a scattering of shags and seagulls rested on isolated rails and derelict posts. A strong salt tang of discarded seaweed was evidence of recently cleaned nets.

Mr Cox greeted us outside his simple stone dwelling with a jug of cool water that he had run off from his tank. But even as we were slaking our thirsts I had my eyes on a nearby apricot tree that was loaded with fruit, much of which was ripe. Mr Cox must have seen our astonished gapes because he said immediately that we could have as much of the fruit as we wished so long as we didn't damage the tree.

No second invitation was needed. Apricots were fruit not in great supply at Fairbridge so after tossing our haversacks under the shade of the tree, we settled down to an unexpected feast.

Later in the afternoon we slipped out of our clothes and splashed about in the water. Away in the distance, the other side of the estuary was just visible through the haze, and there was not a sail on that wide expanse. We were all alone in a tiny backwater paradise where fish and fruit could be had for the taking. And when the wind-chopped water turned grey in the twilight, a flight of pelicans circled in to land with a graceful precision that deserved a bigger audience.

Before it grew dark, Mr Cox allowed us to boil our billy in a makeshift campfire, and after brewing the special issue of tea, we retired to our selected spot to eat our meal. And what better place to enjoy it than underneath the shelter of the apricot tree.

We had already fixed up a rough bed, so when the meal was over we were practically straight into it. We had been advised to have an early night in preparation for a long hard day ahead.

I don't know what it was, but when I awakened in the middle of the night, I instinctively knew that something had happened. Had I heard a noise? Had someone spoken? Still half asleep, I couldn't tell. But whatever it was it had me awake in a few seconds.

I called softly to the others, 'Dick...Stan?'

Someone stirred. 'What's the matter?' In the darkness I recognised Stan's voice.

'I dunno...something woke me up. Are you there Dick?'

No answer.

I felt around but found an empty groundsheet.

'Dick's gone', I said, 'His bed's empty.'

Stan was wide awake now. 'Are you there Dick?' he called. We held our breath and listened. In a few moments a faintly distorted voice answered, 'Yea?'

'Where are you? What's the matter?'

'It's all right, I'm up here.' The sound was directly above us. It went on: 'I felt a bit hungry. I'm having a snack.'

Stan and I remained silent for a few moments until the incongruity of the situation hit us simultaneously. Then we broke out in a fit of laughter. It was unbelievable. Here it was, in the middle of the night, and Dick was up an apricot tree having a feed. He never lived that episode down, and for as long as we were at Fairbridge he was known as 'Dick Darrington, the Midnight Raider'.

The next morning Mr Cox woke us up with a shout: 'There's a brew here if you want it!' Did we want it? It was unheard of, being woken up with a cup of tea. Scrambling out from beneath the apricot tree we made for the house. On the verandah was a small table on which stood three steaming mugs of tea, a big sugar basin and a couple of teaspoons. Giving ourselves liberal serves of sugar, we squatted down on the bare earth slurping at the hot tea to the accompaniment of the sea birds. The gulls were out and about in search of breakfast, while the pelicans cruised around in the morning-calm shallows occasionally dropping their long beaks with an exaggerated nod of the head to scoop an unwary fish.

Through the open door of the cottage the smell of frying sausages accompanied by a pleasant sizzling sound made us forget the birds and got us thinking about ourselves. Then as though in answer to our collective thoughts, a gruff voice pierced the sizzle.

'Better get that tea down ya 'cause yer breakfast is nearly ready'. We couldn't believe our luck. The invitation had scarcely been made before we were on our feet and arranging ourselves on kerosene cases around a rough wooden kitchen table. On its surface were a glass salt and pepper set, a partly emptied bottle of tomato sauce, and a slab of Sunny West butter half-open in its wrapper.

Sitting on the fringes of the Metters No. 2 stove was a scatter of plates each of which held a combination of sausages and eggs. Mr Cox carried one of the plates to the head of the table and sat down. Then waving his left arm towards the stove he said, 'Get stuck into it before the blowies get to it, and there's more tea in the pot'.

Pausing only to blurt out a quick thankyou, we each selected a plate, reseated ourselves and tucked in. Suddenly pushing his chair back, Mr Cox walked briskly to a sideboard and returned to the table with a loaf of bread and a long-bladed knife. 'Forgot the bloody toast', he exclaimed in annoyance, and vigorously set about cutting half a dozen thick slices of bread, then made another quick trip to the sideboard and returned with a jar of marmalade.

'You'll need somethin' to put on it', he explained. And in an afterthought he pointed to the fireplace where a twisted three-pronged length of wire hung on a nail. 'There's the toaster.'

Stan Trigg was already on his way towards the fire with a couple of slices of bread. Opening up the sliding front doors of the stove, he skewered one of the slices with the fork and held it against the coals. After his toast was done, Dick and I followed in quick succession. With marmalade on the table, there was no way we were going to pass up an opportunity like this. At Fairbridge, marmalade was a luxury reserved for Cottage Mothers only.

The night under the tree in the salt-laden air had sharpened our appetites so we did full justice to Mr Cox's hospitality, and when he stacked the bread-scraped plates together, his stubbled face broke into a satisfied grin: 'With the walk you've got ahead of ya, you'll need some decent tucker under yer belts.'

We certainly had that 'under our belts'. I glanced over my brown arms and legs and developing body. 'Little-un' they'd called me back in Eastcombe. If only they could see me now.

Remembering that we were boy scouts and not forgetting

the undreamt-of breakfast, we washed the dishes before packing our gear for the day's march. But Mr Cox hadn't finished with us yet. Fossicking round the watertank stand, he came up with three empty bottles and filled them with water. As he plugged each bottle with a scrap of broken net float he said, 'It's going to be a long hot day; you'll need every drop of this, and for Christ's sake don't lose yer hats. I'm coming with ya to the top of the ridge. Then yer on yer own.'

Stacking the bottles away in our haversacks, we looked up to find Mr Cox already striding towards the western edge of his clearing. The bush was thick and thorny with a fair sprinkling of small banksias. We were happy enough to let him lead the way although we made plenty of noise. We'd been in Australia long enough to know that snakes were timid animals and kept well clear of noise, although there was still a slight danger walking through the bush in bare feet.

For an hour we battled on making steady progress up the rise, and just when the crest seemed never to arrive, we burst into a small clearing and there it was. About two kilometres distant, stretching to the north, south and west horizons was the brilliant deep blue of the Indian Ocean. We paused for a minute or two taking in the magnificent view; surely no other stretch of ocean could be a richer colour. It was Mr Cox who broke the magic of the moment.

'There it is boys. When ya get to the beach, head north until ya meet up with the rest of yer mates on Halls Head.' Then with handshakes all round and prolific thanks from us, he disappeared into the scrub. We were alone.

It took us another hour to reach the beach and we celebrated by stripping off and diving into the surf. A few minutes later we felt refreshed enough to start our trek.

We had hoped that the sand at the water's edge would be firm enough for easy walking, but this happened so infrequently that most of the going was through loose sand, which was not only tiring but soon had us reaching for our bottles of water. By the time the sun was directly overhead we were ready to look for a shady spot in which to rest.

When we came to eat the last of our sandwiches, we found that they had dried out so much that it took most of the remaining water to wash them down. At that stage we weren't too concerned about our water supply, reckoning that another two hours at the most would see us safely back.

But we hadn't accounted for the extra distance that the winding coastline took us. Furthermore, with the hottest part of the day now with us, the rest of our water was soon gone. We trod wearily to reach headland after headland fully expecting to see our people around each one, but disappointment followed every search. And still we plodded on; there was no alternative. With our throats parched we kept our mouths closed in an effort to keep out the hot dry air.

Then at last... faint voices. High pitched children's voices at play struggled to reach us against the stiff sou'-westerly breeze. Automatically we quickened our pace, somehow finding reserves of strength that propelled us towards the drinking water that we knew must accompany the others. I scanned the beach ahead and there it was. Nestling beside a tall sandhill was the water wagon, a piece of driftwood propping up its shafts and the horse standing quietly nearby.

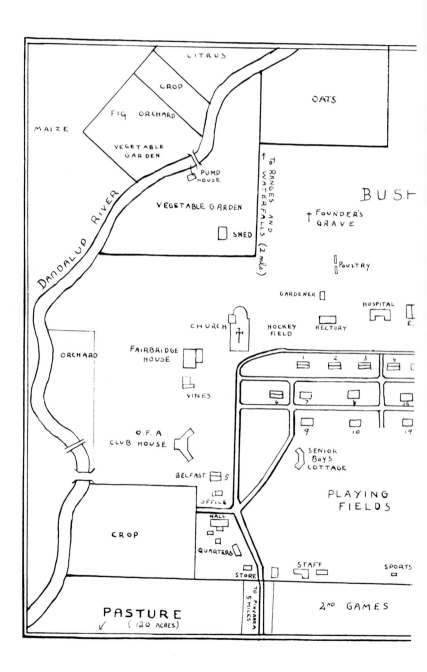

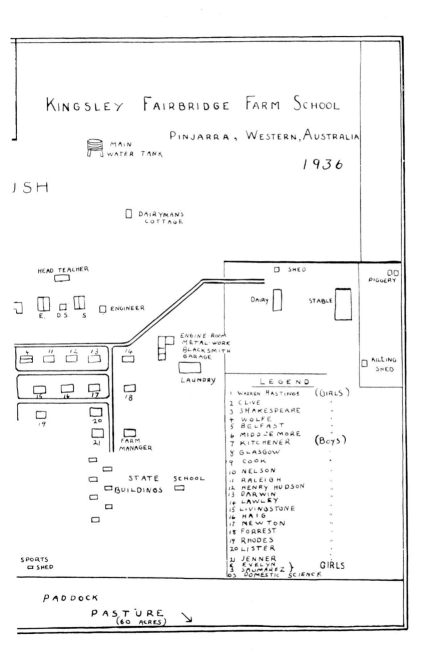

KINGSLEY FAIRBRIDGE FARM SCHOOL

PINJARRA, WESTERN, AUSTRALIA

1936

MAIN WATER TANK

J S H

DAIRYMANS COTTAGE

HEAD TEACHER

E. D S S ENGINEER

SHED

PIGGERY

DAIRY STABLE

4 11 12 13 14

ENGINE ROOM
METAL WORK
BLACKSMITH
GARAGE

KILLING SHED

LAUNDRY

15 16 17 18

19 20

21 FARM MANAGER

STATE SCHOOL BUILDINGS

SPORTS SHED

LEGEND

1 WARREN HASTINGS (GIRLS)
2 CLIVE "
3 SHAKESPEARE "
4 WOLFE "
5 BELFAST "
6 MIDDLEMORE "
7 KITCHENER (BOYS)
8 GLASGOW "
9 COOK "
10 NELSON "
11 RALEIGH "
12 HENRY HUDSON "
13 DARWIN "
14 LAWLEY "
15 LIVINGSTONE "
16 HAIG "
17 NEWTON "
18 FORREST "
19 RHODES "
20 LISTER "
21 JENNER "
22 EVELYN }
23 SJUMAREZ } GIRLS
DS DOMESTIC SCIENCE

PADDOCK

PASTURE
(60 ACRES)

FAIRBRIDGE SENIORS

Standard seven and eight children at Fairbridge in the mid-30s were fortunate in having some excellent school teachers, particularly Mr Reg Spear and Mr Vic Nelson.

Mr Spear immediately wore the nickname 'Prod', a tag to which he took some exception. In this regard he and I had a great deal in common, which perhaps influenced my attitude towards him. However the ability in handling the joint problem of name-calling was decidedly in his favour. Whereas he had the persuasive power of the metre-long cane to support his authoritative attempts to silence his tormentors, my armoury was bare. The wise cowards consequently resorted to restricting their barbs to occasions when Mr Spear was well out of earshot.

For all that, he was a popular teacher and an even more popular man. He always made himself available after school to listen to any problem a boy might have, whether it be academic or personal. His was a face of understanding; sympathetic eyes which, behind a bent nose, added wisdom to his intelligence, were augmented by a slightly jutting chin. He would listen with patience and counsel with skill. He was a boy's man.

Every morning Mr Spear held a period of current topics to keep his class informed of world events. As he owned one of the few wireless sets in the village giving him access to global news, he was well informed on this subject. And there was so much happening around the world that I couldn't wait to get to school for the next exciting chapter. The news had everything; drama, excitement, adventure and tragedy. How anyone could regard history as being a dull subject was beyond my comprehension. There was no doubt about it in my opinion, we were living in fascinating times and Mr Spear brought it all to life on the blackboard.

With the coastline of Burma occupying a semi-permanent position on one board, we followed the forlorn search for Australia's famous aviator Charles Kingsford-Smith who was missing somewhere in the region. Day after day we settled into our desks hoping for news of his survival, until one morning the news that a plane's wheel had been washed up sent the classroom into gloom. There were plenty of other disturbing events happening around the world too. It was 1937, my last year at school.

Japan had invaded China and there were reports of wholesale slaughter in the city of Nanking where Japanese soldiers had massacred a hundred-thousand Chinese civilians, mostly women and children. There was concern too about a new German Chancellor by the name of Adolf Hitler who was re-arming his country and sending Europe into turmoil.

Then there came the sensational abdication of our new King before he had even been crowned. The news stunned Fairbridge with its traditional ties to the throne. Cottage Mothers talked of nothing else for days while our teachers explained the implications of the crisis.

On the other hand, Australia and England were periodically locked in battles of a different nature, which although lasting only a few days at a time, were none the less furiously fought. The names of famous battlefields like Trent Bridge, Old Trafford, The Oval and Lords dominated our current affairs periods and sometimes spilled well over into less important subjects all through the English summer. Good-natured banter fluctuated with the fortunes of each side, and although the teachers were heavily outnumbered, they sportingly took our gloating very well.

Whenever possible, Mr Spear opened the window of his

quarters to let a few of his class listen to the fascinating static of a ball-by-ball description of the test matches, but unfortunately the timing allowed only a brief period of this treat in the evenings.

Although teachers and students displayed different loyalties over cricket teams, we joined forces in order to produce an Australian Rules football team. To begin with we British-born boys ridiculed the idea of trying to play a game of 'football' by controlling the oval-shaped object with the hands. As far as we were concerned, a ball was a sphere and a sphere was a globe with every point equi-distant from the centre. But the persistence of Mr Healey, Mr Spear and a bright young new teacher, Mr Vic Nelson, gradually dismantled the barriers of prejudice. Blackboards displayed large oval shapes on which unfamiliar positional places were written and explained. The functions of rucks, rovers, half-forwards and goalsneaks were demonstrated along with the controversial rule of holding the man or ball. A squad of senior boys was chosen for mid-week tuition and gradually our enthusiasm increased. Ball-handling techniques, drop kicks and punts were taught as well as positioning, leading and tackling. The scoring took a bit of getting used to after the soccer game, particularly the custom of presenting a consolation prize when the tall sticks were missed. Perseverance paid off however, and scratch matches were used to eliminate faults and correct mistakes, especially the undisciplined habit of everyone chasing the ball like a howling pack of wolves.

But when captains were appointed and discipline tightened, the standard improved, permitting the skills of the game to bring some satisfaction to our long-suffering coaches. Eventually a team was selected and a game organised against Pinjarra school.

This was just the incentive we needed. From then on the chosen side trained on every possible occasion; the reputation of the school was at stake, and even though we weren't expected to win, we desperately wanted to put up a fighting performance.

It was no coincidence that our star player was made

captain. Not only was Ernie Skippings a champion athlete, he was built like a whippet and had a cat-like leap. No one at Fairbridge could outmark Ernie; we hoped that Pinjarra stars went equally markless. But a tough game seemed assured. After all they had cut their teeth on it — we were still sucking the dummy.

Nevertheless, as we trotted out onto our sportsground in singlets and shorts our spirits were high despite being confronted with a side immaculately turned out in spotless strip including boots. The human brain has the happy knack of forgetting the details of life's defeats and because I have no memory of the result there is a distinct possibility that we lost.

Over the years these football matches became regular fixtures with the Pinjarra school, as indeed did the girls' hockey matches and other sports. We at Fairbridge valued them greatly, not only for the competition but also for the generous supply of oranges the opposing teams brought with them.

But despite the extra vitamins and the benefit of Mr Nelson's coaching I lost my position as champion junior athlete to Jock Paterson that year. The only event I won was the long jump, no doubt as the result of conjuring images of bright green snakes being dragged from their holes. There was some satisfaction in us being both in the same faction, but that still didn't stop Red faction from winning the shield.

With the winter sports over, interest focused on the season's swimming chiefly because Fairbridge had a brand new pool. In 1936 a gentleman by the name of Mr Broadhurst had donated 200 pounds to enable the river to be dammed just behind the Club House. The result was a magnificent swimming pool more than two-hundred-and-fifty metres long, and complete with diving board and dressing sheds. Now Mr Branson had a suitable stretch of water in which to conduct his swimming lessons. He taught dozens of children right through to Bronze Medallion standard.

Popular though swimming was, cricket was still the dominant summer game amongst the boys. Occasionally matches were arranged between neighbouring towns and an Old Fairbridgian side if there were enough of them holidaying at the Clubhouse. This gave incentive to make the school team and naturally made for a more fierce inter-cottage competition.

Once again there were all-round champions with Ernie Skippings taking over where Harry Lucas had left off now that he was out in the workforce. Ernie was not only our best Aussie Rules player, but he had won the Senior Athlete medal and was also one of the best cricketers.

But bracketed with him on the cricket pitch was Henry McCaughan. Henry was a nuggety Irishman with a typical lyrical brogue which fascinated me. But what impressed me more was his skill and aggression with the cricket bat, for he was one Irishman who took great delight in reserving his paddy to slaughter opposing bowlers. And it was no joke facing up to his own fast deliveries whenever Rhodes played Isaac Newton. But once he'd thrashed us on the cricket field, that was the end of it. The rest of the time we were the best of mates, a situation I found most rewarding.

Most of the boys in the same classroom knocked about together on the school grounds particularly after dinner when there was time to get a game of something going. But during the short recess when Henry and I might have been having a bit of catching practice, a most attractive girl seemed quite keen to join in and always stood close to him. It was only a matter of time before I realised they were sweethearts, a fact that I found most agreeable especially when I discovered that she was from Scotland.

Now I had the privilege of being friends with an Irishman and a Scots lass, a combination of voices that sounded to me more tuneful than some duets I'd heard. But as pleasant as the association was to start with, I soon realised that this sparkle-eyed lass was sending me into a spin. The problem was of course that she was my best friend's girl and I was far too young to understand the eternal triangle syndrome. Nevertheless, that is what it was and there was nothing I could do about it other than break up a good friendship which I was not qualified to do. So in turn, I suffered, agonised, became enraptured, despaired and prayed in silence. At almost fifteen years of age, it was my first experience of turmoil, of passion, and the trauma of obsessive infatuation. I was trapped, hopelessly ensnared. I survived on the occasional glance, the brief residue of a smile, the thrill of the gentlest of touches, and the sound of her voice. The agony of it all was that I could not openly respond; emotion had to be checked and words carefully censored. Yet through it all I was a willing slave. If we were in church, or attending a school's broadcast in the club house, I positioned myself so that I could sneak an unobtrusive glance in the hope of catching her eye. If by chance our eyes met, it was enough to set my heart pounding. I certainly gave myself a hard time.

In 1936 a change had been made to the school's curriculum. As the result of a conference between Colonel Heath, Mr Healey and the Education Department of Western Australia, boys in their last year of schooling (up to fourteen years and nine months), were given vocational training for one week in three. Much of this training came in very useful in later life; other jobs were purely functional and necessary for the effective running of the institution.

For instance, Mrs Green the staff kitchen's sole caterer needed three boy assistants to prepare vegetables, clean the dining room, set the tables and wash the dishes. At mealtimes, one boy waited on the tables calling the orders through a servery, while the other two brought the meals to him from the stove.

The disagreeable part of this job was the need for an early start to have the two stove fires well established before Mrs Green's arrival. Not that she had to come far; her quarters adjoined the kitchen, but experience taught us that if her entrance coincided with a healthy burst of steam from a friendly kettle, the day's disasters could be faced with a little extra toleration.

And considering her work load, Mrs Green needed all the tolerance she had, especially when she was called on to arbitrate between two selfish staff members fighting over the last serve of Welsh Rarebit.

In three minutes flat this energetic little woman had the morning's first pot of tea made and poured, and with the empty teapot still in her hand came the curt instruction.

'Come along you boys, you're tea's poured out', and if I happened to be in the dining room out of earshot, she'd call from the servery, 'Did you hear me Ramsbottom? Stop whatever you're doing and come and have your tea.'

That was typical of Mrs Green: a small bundle of efficiency working to a tight schedule, yet always finding time to look after her boys. Again, after the last person had left the dining room, her power-packed command came through loud and clear: 'Close the door Ramsbottom and come and have your breakfast.'

Breakfast for the kids on staff dining-room duties was a fantasy of food. It started with real oatmeal porridge with plenty of hot milk and an unrationed measure of sugar, or alternatively, a plate of Weeties or Cornflakes. This was followed by a choice of whatever had been on the menu with even the eggs cooked to one's choosing, after which there was any amount of marmalade on toast and cups of tea.

And it didn't stop with breakfast. Lunch and tea were equally satisfying. Mrs Green fed us on whatever the staff ate, only more of it. These perks more than outweighed the late finish each evening, an unavoidable necessity because the working staff and the teachers had to be fed. It was usually seven o'clock before we knocked off, but this was compensated for by a two-and-a-half-hour break during the afternoon. And of course it was a seven-day-a-week job, but even this inconvenience meant that church parade was missed.

On the other hand, working in the main kitchen was sheer drudgery with none of the perks of the staff kitchen, although, because the evening meal was eaten in the cottages, work usually finished for the day mid-way through the afternoon. But not before the great volume of greasy dishes and big pots had been washed and inspected. And if a band member on main kitchen duty thought that he might be treated more leniently by Mr Shugar, he was very much mistaken. The one thing that he insisted upon more than any other was the necessity for a high standard of cleanliness.

Perhaps the only dubious benefit the main kitchen worker had, was the constant stirring of a forty-litre pot of porridge over a huge range fire on a bitterly cold morning, but only after a five o'clock rise.

Tucked in behind the main dining hall was the bakehouse. A long, low building with a spacious oven at one end, it had the capacity to bake two hundred one-kilogram loaves per day. Here again, it was a five o'clock start for two boys, mixing the dough in a long wooden trough, after which it was covered with bags and left for several hours to rise. Then in the early afternoon, the dough was weighed, kneaded and placed into the baking tins where it would remain for another hour. During this time the oven would be brought to the correct temperature before raking out the fire. A long-handled spatula was then used to place the tins to the back of the oven until they were all in and the door closed. After a further hour, a test was made and if satisfactory, the batch was retrieved and the loaves tipped out and stacked.

I can well remember having my after-school trombone tuition interrupted by the head bakery boy handing Mr Shugar a double upright loaf for approval, whereupon he would inspect it for colour, tap it in several places and smell it before handing it back apparently satisfied. And of course, there was always enough dough mixed for the little rolls that were put aside for a later snack along with the jam and anything else that could be scrounged.

There couldn't have been too much wrong with the baking at Fairbridge because the farm school was a consistent winner in the baking section at the Pinjarra Show.

Most of the vocational training labour was absorbed in the hectares of vegetable gardens and orchard. These were spread over a wide expanse of rich river loam on both sides of the river behind the church. An elaborate sprinkler system ensured an all-year supply of a big variety of vegetables, enough to meet the requirements of the whole school. A large tin shed in the centre of the gardens housed mixed bags of fertilizers, wheelbarrows and tools and also served as a store-room for crops such as onions and pumpkins.

The architect of this vast project was a dumpy little man, middle-aged and balding, who lived with his wife and twin daughters in a cottage overlooking his landscape patchwork panorama. A perfectionist in everything he did, he was seen to advantage guiding his single-furrowed plough with immaculate accuracy through a patch of fallow, the gleaming red of the freshly turned earth contrasting sharply with the grey of the old mare.

Mr Brain also had a dozen or so boys to help him and he saw to it that no one was idle for very long. If there wasn't hoeing to be done there were carrots to be thinned out, fertilizer to mix, vegetables to pick and always weeding of seed beds needed; most of them being boring, tedious and repetitive jobs, especially for teenage boys who would far sooner be roaming wild pinging at parrots with home made gings.

A job in the big shed was the thing to aim for, not that there were too many going there especially for the smaller boys. While they were despatched to distant fields, the more robust- looking types mixed carefully measured quantities of superphosphate, blood and bone, sulphate of ammonia, copper, sulphate and potash for the next planting. And being under supervision, it was fairly constant work, but regular spells could be engineered by asking a pertinent question or two at selected times. This ruse not only gained a breather, but it also enhanced the prospects of being asked to 'slip up for morning tea will you Ramsbottom?'

This didn't mean that there was morning tea on for everyone. No such amenities existed in those days. It was purely a request to go to his house and fetch the morning tea that his wife had prepared for him. But Mrs Brain was a woman of compassion who always sent back a tray laden with extra hot water and milk plus a plate of home cooking far in excess of her husband's needs. And we were allowed to rest while Mr Brain refreshed himself.

His every mouthful of tea or scone or cake was watched with ever-growing concern, particularly on a cold day when his appetite reached alarming proportions which threatened to thwart his good wife's intentions by forgetting the basic rule of etiquette of leaving something on his plate. However, more often than not he would rise from his garden chair with a gesture towards the remaining food and say, 'You boys might as well finish this off', and leave us to it.

And even then, there was a certain protocol to observe; there was no such thing as a mad scramble. The first preference went to the delivery boy, after which a definite pecking order was followed in order of seniority. The junior boys rarely got a look in, not that they became too distressed; they knew their turn would come.

The least desirable work came under the heading of 'general duties'. When the vocational trainees formed up in front of the church for job distribution there was always a fear of being detailed for this. In military fashion, Bonk inspected the ranks like the commander he was, peeling off parties with precision until all who remained knew they were destined for general duties. And with a place the size of Fairbridge, there was always maintenance to be done.

But if anyone thought that he was safe from detection by working in some secluded spot, he was destined for a shock. Bonk was known to climb the church bell tower from where he had a commanding view over most of the village with a vocal capacity guaranteed to reach every corner. The stories of his exploits were legendary; passed down from generation to generation like battle honours in the history of the regiment.

It is alleged that the Colonel in his lofty perch for half an hour, watched a lad sitting on the bank of a drain he was supposed to be cleaning. A broadside from the tower sent the boy scurrying into activity. Confronting him later, Bonk asked the quivering lad what he was doing sitting down.

'Resting, sir', came the frightened reply.

'Well', boomed the Colonel, 'in future when you are doing your resting you will lie flat on your back, then I shall know exactly when you are supposed to be working.'

The favourite story that went the rounds told of the time that Bonk spotted two wags returning from the direction of the river shortly after a church service. Asked for an explanation, they said they had gone for a walk immediately after church.

'Very well', said Bonk. 'Perhaps you will be good enough to tell me what hymns we had this morning?'

This had the boys floundering for a few seconds until one of them blurted out. 'I remember now sir, they were *Abide With Me* and *Rock of Ages*.'

'Is that so', mused Bonk. 'In that case at five o'clock this evening you will abide with me in my office, and I shall see that you rock for ages afterwards.'

I knew from experience that that was no idle threat. I'd been caught stealing grapes from a vine near the teachers' quarters, and reported directly to the Colonel. As usual I had to report to him at the appointed hour to hear the dreaded order. 'Get them down lad!'

Trembling with fear, I dropped my short pants and leant over a chair. Bonk may have had only one arm, but it seemed to me that in that one he possessed the strength of two, and a half a dozen lashes later I knew all about it.

The following day I came face to face with him again when I took Mrs Green's menu to the office for typing. 'Can you sit down today lad?' he queried. Foolishly I said, 'Yes, sir'.

'That's a pity. I shall have to put a bit more weight into it next time.' But there was not to be a next time. Shortly after that incident, Colonel Heath left the school to administer the new Fairbridge Farm School at Bacchus Marsh in Victoria. The school was genuinely sorry to see him go. He had served the Fairbridge Farm School at Pinjarra for over eight years during which time some six hundred children had passed through the scheme under his guidance. As with all disciplinarians, he had a standard from which he never budged, and once it was accepted, the school functioned at its peak.

Before he left he paid the band a last visit, thanking Mr Shugar for his remarkable achievement and us members for our contribution to the good reputation that the school enjoyed throughout the State. As the Colonel and his family drove slowly through the cheering ranks of children, the band played its final tribute from outside the main dining hall

Colonel and Mrs. Heath, with their daughter and the family dog.

from which old Bonk had issued so many instructions, delivered countless speeches, and had introduced more than a few famous personalities among whom had been the Duke and Duchess of York (later to become King George the sixth and the Queen of England), the Duke of Gloucester, the poet laureate John Masefield, and the distinguished cricketer C.B. Fry.

To the strains of *Will Ye No Come Back Again* the Colonel's car shuddered over the cattle pit and disappeared in a cloud of red dust up to the half-mile bend and beyond. One thing to remember though, was that a child's personal file wasn't wiped clean with the arrival of a new Principal. And there was a period of unsettlement after Colonel Heath's departure. Mr Paterson's term of Principal lasted only a year before he was succeeded by Canon Watson who was also the padre.

Soon after the Canon's appointment he introduced compulsory morning prayers in the chapel. This meant that although the actual prayer time was only ten minutes, a total of half an hour's cleaning time was lost, an imposition that did not endear the reverend gentleman to his youthful flock. For my part I preferred to compose my own prayers and say them silently in the sanctuary of my bed and restrict them to modest requests, like a personal spectacular performance in the next sporting fixture. My only plea for a miracle was for the lovely Christina to take my hand in hers, reduce me to delirium with her bewitching eyes, and beg me to be her boyfriend.

The fact that neither prayer nor miracle was answered sowed the first seeds of doubt in my mind as to the authenticity of divine intervention.

But it was not all disappointment. On the contrary, as a senior boy at Fairbridge, life became increasingly more interesting. In the summer of 1937, Mr Healey took a selected carload of cottage captains to Perth for the day to watch a combined Australian team play the touring Englishmen at the W.A.C.A. ground. Not since my first Weston-Super-Mare outing had I been so excited. It was more than a dream come true; it was a miracle — perhaps sent as a substitute for my unrequited love.

But what thrilled me most about the outing was the possibility of seeing two of Gloucestershire's famous cricketers in action. Charlie Barnett and the great Wally Hammond were in the party and I hoped they would be included in the team.

In addition to my own personal interest, there was a tremendous amount of national feeling about this series. This was the first English tour after the sensational bodyline tests, and it was being looked on as an unofficial reconciliation tour, with a great deal of goodwill to be made up between the two nations.

The weekend before, the Englishmen had scored a comfortable win over a Western Australian side starting with a score of 469 for 4. However, with the inclusion of some pretty useful Eastern Staters in Grimmet, McCabe, Fingleton and Babcock, the combined team was expected to put up far stiffer resistance.

But we had to wait for our moment of glory. Mr Healey had organised a trip to Maylands aerodrome before the match, which normally would have been the highlight of a boy's day out. To be given the chance to inspect the planes and even a flight over the city was an opportunity not to be missed. Yet today, because of the big-time cricket, not one of us was willing to risk our necks in case an accident robbed us of the chance to see our heroes.

And although it was interesting enough talking to a pilot and sitting in the cockpit of a bi-plane, none of us was really happy until we were sitting behind the wicket at the southern end of the ground waiting for the action to start. It was only a minor disappointment when Australia won the toss and decided to bat. I had hoped for the reverse to happen so that I could have seen Wally Hammond at the crease; instead, Babcock and Horrocks stayed in for most of the day scoring a century each. But because of Bill Voce's long run-up, we did get a good view of the distinctive pumping action of his delivery. All in all it was a memorable day, one to talk about for weeks ahead, and to remember for a lifetime.

Back at school for the final term, both Mr Spear and Mr Healey displayed their experience in handling the senior class. Mr Spear introduced us to Shakespeare through *Midsummer Night's Dream* and *The Merchant of Venice* which added a little culture to an otherwise modest standard of education. On the other hand, Mr Healey's personal wartime service more than qualified him to take us in modern history. Inevitably, when he warmed to his subject, the lesson reverted to fascinating stories of warfare in the trenches and life in the villages of Belgium and France, particularly around the village of 'Wipers', as it was known. But for all his wartime exploits, he would never tell us how he became wounded. Whatever the cause, it left him with a permanent limp.

My extra-curricular school activity during my final months was being the weather man. This entailed a daily reading of the rain gauge, estimating the wind force and direction, and the type and degree of cloud cover, and recording it on a special form to be sent to the Meteorological Department at the end of each month. It was a simple enough task really, the only slight inconvenience being to remember the readings on the weekends.

Another interest I had that year was to play a minor part in manufacturing a mast, boom and sail for a syndicate of us to use at the next Mandurah camp. This work was done under the supervision of Reg Edwards, who, apart from being the bass drummer in the band, was mad keen on the Navy and anything to do with sailing. The plan was for four of us to pool our financial resources in order to hire a boat during the holidays. In the meantime we spent some time in shaping the boom and mast out of saplings and forging the U-shaped marrying bracket in the metalwork shop. Somehow Reg got hold of a nice piece of canvas which he cut into a mainsail. He was fortunate in working in the engine room and having a sympathetic engineer to encourage him in the project. Mr J.B. Young not only maintained the newly installed Rushton engine that supplied the village with power, but was also the electrician. In Reg he had a willing pupil who was competent enough to supervise the engine room while he himself attended to other jobs, so between them they had a pretty good working relationship. I think it must have been Mr Young who bought the eyelets for the sail, but it was Reg who sewed them in. And it was probably Mr Young again who gave Reg the pulleys, but we were to wait until we got to Mandurah to buy suitable rope for the halyard. Our big project now was the raising of funds for the hire of the boat and for general expenses.

After a meeting of the 'crew', it was decided to have a bottle drive with an all out assault on the workers' quarters. When they were made aware of the situation, they co-operated to such an extent that we were able to send to Pinjarra, on the school's utility, a total of twelve dozen empties which netted us six shillings. With the boat hire charges of ten shillings per week it was a good start. We hoped Christmas would be kind and supply us with the balance. Christmas was very kind to me that year, although no money was involved, it brought me a letter from my mother. It is the only one of her letters that I have still.

Bismore Eastcombe
Nr. Stroud Glos.
England

Dear Jack

I hope this finds you well, we are very well just now. I was glad to hear you are doing well with your schooling - learn all you can. I have had one of my old boys home to see us, one I brought up from a baby of 6 months old. Now he is married and has 3 children but we was very pleased to see them — they are now living in London. Florence too has been home — she has now come back to Shipton Moine Nr. Tetbury Glos. She works on a farm and I think that suits her better than house work and John Bottomley paid us a visit at August Bank Holiday but George Brown I've not seen since he has been out of work he is rather a long way off so cannot afford to come yet but he wants to very bad but I am not able to send his fare so of course he has got to wait. We are having our Harvest Festavle next Sunday that makes us think we shall soon have winter and you will be having your summer wont you you will be surprised to know that I now have one little boy the other two have gone back. I do not expect to have any more in their place. I begin to find they are too much for me so that I cannot do the work for them now I must close with best of good wishes

from your loving
Mother and Dad

Florence and John Bottomley were brother and sister who had been brought up by Mother before my time, but I had seen them occasionally on their visits back to Bismore.

FAIRBRIDGE FARM SCHOOLS INC.
SAVOY HOUSE, STRAND, LONDON, W.C.2

21 APR 1938

The following _HALF YEARLY PROGRESS_ Report, dated _21st Dec. 1937._ has been received from the Kingsley Fairbridge Farm School, Western Australia.

Name_JACK K. RAMSBOTTOM._ Date of birth_12.11.22._ Party_May, 1933._

COTTAGE   Arthur Scratton.   SCHOOL STANDARD   11 A.

COTTAGE MASTER'S REPORT: A quiet boy, very willing and obedient, with a pleasant disposition.   His character has improved steadily in Scratton and with a good start he should do well.
                    G.S.Greenish.

STATE SCHOOL REPORT:
English.   Conduct   V.Good.
  Composition V.Good.   Progress   "
  Spelling   "   Remarks: Has ability and is a great worker.
  Writing   "   R.S.Spear.   Head Teacher.
  Literature   "
Arithmetic.
  Mental   "
  Written   "
  Mensuration   "
Social Subjects "
Drawing   Good.

GENERAL HEALTH REPORT: Excellent health.   Satisfactory progress.
Height 61½" Weight 108 lbs. H. MacDonald. Nursing Sister.

ACTING PRINCIPAL'S REMARKS: Good boy.
                    WALTER H. WATSON.

The General Superintendent,
The Migration Department,
Dr. Barnardo's Homes

Jack Ramsbottom's school report, 1937.

202

WORKING THE FARM

With 1937 coming to a close and my final year's exams passed, my schooldays were over and it was time to move into the senior quarters. Shortly after my arrival in 1933, Wellington had been pulled down and a magnificent new building for the senior boys had been built. It comprised two wings of sixteen separated cubicles each, built on an angle out from the central hub of living quarters for the cottage parents and kitchen, dining room and bathrooms for the boys. But the feature of the place was a central clock tower with its four-sided face that could be seen throughout the village.

So my new quarters was cubicle number 24 in the Arthur Scratton Memorial Building, so named after the donor of the money to build it.

My new Cottage Parents were Mr and Mrs Greenish whose ten-year-old daughter lived with them but went to school in Pinjarra. Mr Greenish was a short balding man of fifty with a lined and tanned face weathered from the result of a score or more years' service in the Navy. Mrs Greenish was a gentle, mild-mannered little woman who went about her work in a quiet, efficient and considerate manner.

My entry into Scratton was the start of a new chapter in my life. No longer were we boys, we were young men, and Mrs Greenish treated us like it. Seated now at the long central table in the main dining hall, I looked across to Miss

Rice and her Rhodes boys with a feeling of intense satisfaction, of smugness, that at last I was no longer subjected to the unpredictable behaviour of children. A new attitude existed in Scratton, a new direction, a step towards manhood. Although, of necessity, discipline was still maintained, the sheer repetitive monotony of cottage life was behind me for ever. Just having a room of my own, small though it may have been, was of tremendous psychological importance in shaping the future.

For the first time since I had been taken from my foster parents, I had four walls to myself, a room of my very own, my own desk, and more importantly, only one bed — my bed. Among my few possessions that I had brought from Rhodes was a black and white drawing that had won first prize in its category at the last school show. I had copied it from the cover of *The Broadcaster* that Mr Spear had brought to school to give us inspiration. The caricature depicted a tearful male singer performing in front of a microphone, while a spaniel in evening dress mopped up a pool of tears. At Mr Spear's suggestion, I had captioned the drawing 'Bing', a title that was meaningless to me at the time, but subsequently became a familiar and enjoyable personality in my life.

With great care, I selected a position above my desk and pinned the picture onto a wall stud. I then stood back, not so much to admire it, but rather as an act of declaring my territory, something akin to a male dog's cocking of the leg. Whatever it was, this small room was a place where I could close the door and call it home.

I was also now a member of the permanent work force which meant working on what was termed the 'farm side'. The practical part of Kingsley Fairbridge's overall scheme was about to begin.

The operation of this important section of the Fairbridge Farm School required a number of experienced people, some of them married, many of them single. The married ones lived in cottages on the fringe of the village and included the farm manager Mr Yull, and the dairyman Mr Goulder. The teamster, Mr Mathews, lived with his family independently on a small property in the foothills about a kilometre away. Mr Carter the poultryman and Mr Jack Mann a farm hand, together with itinerate labourers, lived in the staff quarters between the store and the main kitchen. They were the ones who so generously helped with our Mandurah sailing plans.

My first man-sized job was as a dairy hand. I was one of nine boys. For the milk to be delivered to the main and staff kitchens by 7.00am meant that milking had to start by five, and the cows had to be brought in from the paddock first. Two boys took it in turns to do this while the rest of us sauntered sleepily straight to the dairy. For the first few days persuading the milk to drop into the bucket was the least of my problems. I was far more worried about a fully-laden hefty cow plonking its hoof on my cold toes, and the disconcerting, although warm, shower of urine from an excited beast that usually accompanied my tugging on her teats.

But after a few days I was milking as many as the rest of them, and I even had my own pet, 'Goldie'. An understanding throughout the shed made the poaching of another boy's pet because it may have been an easier milker, an unpardonable offence. To my knowledge, a newcomer may have unwittingly breached this code, but it was never done deliberately.

With a shed capacity of eighteen stalls, and one boy working the separator, it took three sheds to get through the herd. And there was no time to waste. At the same time, there was no lowering of hygiene standards. Before each cow was milked the udder had to be washed, and after each milking the bucket was taken straight to the milk room for straining. The cream was reserved for a few selected staff members. In winter time when supplies increased, some went to the staff kitchen.

Before we could knock off for breakfast, the milking shed had to be hosed down and left spotlessly clean. There was no short cut to cleanliness, daily inspections saw to that. So with two hours work done, rumbling stomachs demanded something more substantial than porridge and bread with dripping and jam. The extra rations were usually rissoles which we promptly made into 'buttees', an English term for a sandwich.

After breakfast, calves slurped down the skim milk and the huge bull chewed thoughtfully on his specialised diet. While two or three boys attended to these jobs as well as cleaning the pens, the rest of us were taught how to kill and dress a sheep which included the care and treatment of the skins. In the absence of refrigeration, the carcases were hung in a brush-roofed meat house with walls of fly-proof netting. Built under the shade of a tree, it allowed the breeze to do the cooling without fear of contamination. In the middle of the sawdust-covered floor stood a solid section of tree trunk that served as a chopping block. It was to this structure that the senior girls came with their orders for the staff wives to whom they were apprenticed as domestics. And while Mr Goulder wielded knife and chopper, we boys received a running commentary on the skills of butchering and an explanation on the various cuts of meat, even down to what scraps to give Mrs Healey's cat and dog.

Occasionally a steer was killed which, to me, was not a pleasant task. Having been kept in the executioner's pen overnight, the beast, sensing its impending fate, summoned all its energy in resisting the final few yards to the slaughter site. With terrified eyes it bellowed, it snorted, it lashed out, it dug in. It fought gallantly for its life before sheer weight of numbers dragged it into position for the pistol shot to the brain that would render it senseless. Finally, with its last desperate fight lost, the beast stood dejectedly, resigned, until the cartridge shot sent it collapsing to the ground. Then in an instant, its throat was cut.

Because of the dairy hands' early start, an extended lunch break was permitted, taking us back to work at 2.00pm. During the hour before the afternoon's milking, there was chaff or maize to be cut and supplementary cows' feed to mix which was given to them while they were being milked. I always gave the maize, chaff and bran mixture to my cows on the understanding that they wouldn't kick me. Whether it had any effect on them or not, I didn't know, but so much did they look forward to their afternoon snack that as soon as the gate to the holding yard was opened, exactly the required number would scurry up the ramp into the milking shed. Yet for all their keenness, they knew just what number shed they were in and never tried to jump the queue for fear of missing out on their treat.

The only difference from the morning's routine was that no separating was done, as all the milk was taken by horse and cart to the distribution point outside the dining hall. By the time these two boys returned and unharnessed their horse, the cleaning up was finished which brought their work day to a close.

The other farm side jobs involved working with sheep, horses and men. It wasn't long before I discovered that there was more to the sheep business than drenching, branding, crutching and shearing. For the farm visitor, lambing season is one of the most delightful times of the year; to see wriggling white tails of suckling day-old offspring, the frolic of the same lambs a week later, and the plaintive bleat of the temporary lost, has been the catalyst for poets to scribe; but for the farmer, there has to be a far less appealing role to play.

When they reach a certain age, lambs have to be tailed and many of the males castrated. The method in use in the '30s more than guaranteed to curtail their frolicking, and the plaintive bleats changed dramatically into cries of pain as wriggly tails were lopped with a single swish of a sharp knife. And for the little rams there was worse to come.

One boy held the struggling animal by its four feet, holding left and right legs together, then presented it to the surgeon by resting its backside on the operating table. A quick flash of the knife whipped off the end of the scrotum, leaving the way clear for the removal of the testes. This was done by manoeuvring them through the open wound whereby they could be gripped by the teeth and withdrawn, usually one at a time, to be discarded on the ground. With a little practice, the experienced operator could demonstrate his skill by extracting both testicles together, a feat that never failed to draw a murmur of approval from the onlookers. But none appreciated a day of de-sexing lambs more than the farm dogs.

By contrast, the most popular job on the farm side was working in the stables. With a dozen horses to look after, including a few riding hacks, there was always the chance of a ride. Not that we were ever permitted to ride at will, but occasionally Mr Yull, the farm manager, would take a boy out in the paddocks with him. However, it was never enough to satisfy the normal adventurous spirit of the farm boy. The most we were ever allowed when accompanying Mr Yull was a sedate trot, when what we dreamed of was a full-blooded gallop with the wind whipping the breath away. But this could only be done on the quiet, and then only by the more enterprising boys. They would get up before dawn to be out in the paddocks at first light ready to slip a halter over a hack and set off in a bare-back gallop. There was always the risk of detection of course, but that served only to add spice to the adventure, and Mr Yull was known never to have reported an offender.

The legitimate routine was to round the horses up on foot at 6.00am and give them a thorough grooming with curry-comb and brush. After breakfast, Mr Yull allocated so many boys to each adult worker depending on the work priority. Apart from stables work there was always clearing, fencing and general maintenance to do; the type of work that I was happy enough doing because it took me out to the distant boundaries of the farm, mostly in the bush, swinging an axe or working up a sweat on the end of a crosscut saw.

These were some of my most impressionable days at Fairbridge, particularly when I worked with Mr Jones, a character of a Welshman. With him letting me have the reins, the old dray creaked and groaned its way to the hills for a day of fence mending. The outward journey was pleasant enough with our intelligent draught horse striding along at a fair pace while the eloquent Mr Jones extolled the virtues of his native land. I must admit, I was taken with the lyrical inflection of his voice which blended perfectly with the bird calls of the Australian bush. That is, when things were going smoothly. Slight imperfections of tone and irregularity of speech were to be detected however, if he encountered trivialities such as a stubborn stump or a smashed thumb. I found his flexibility of vocabulary slightly amusing; it added variety to the day. But on occasions throughout the day when a multiplicity of mishaps got the better of him, a dramatic display of versatility threatened the life of anyone in his immediate vicinity only to see him regain his equilibrium with an outbreak of gutsy laughter. Life was not boring. But there came a time when not even his nationalistic humour could save him from losing control.

It happened on the way home while tackling a difficult creek crossing. The dray was loaded with fence posts, coils of wire, an assortment of tools and a host of sundry items. It was not as though Mr Jones was careless; he even had us get off the cart for the crossing. But the task was beyond the strength of our horse. We became bogged. At that stage we were in an unfortunate predicament, which, in my view could have been rectified by lightening the load. But Mr Jones thought otherwise. Not for all the Joneses in Wales was he going to the trouble of unloading all that heavy gear; the bloody horse was being just plain bloody lazy. It was clear to me that Mr Jones was under considerable stress, yet for the first few minutes his demeanour was merely volatile. Time and time again he implored the distressed animal to greater effort so that we could all get home. But with every movement the wheels sank deeper.

After three minutes Mr Jones exploded into a shower of verbal sparks like the dying moments of a spent rocket. All I could do was to stare in amazed yet grudging admiration. By this time the poor animal was on its fore-knees as though praying for divine assistance with Mr Jones tugging at the bit threatening to despatch the so-and-so bastard to its so-and-so maker if it didn't so-and-so hurry up and get out of the so-and-so, so-and-so bog.

The man's vituperation held me spellbound. We had used mild swear words discreetly between each other, but my ears had heard nothing like this before. Mr Jones was clearly a man of letters. I couldn't understand why a person with his qualifications was working as a farm labourer. True, I had heard that 'times were bad', that employment was not easy to find, but surely a man of his linguistic skills could have found a less hazardous job, perhaps somewhere in the diplomatic service. However, I was pleased with myself for not letting the free lesson slip by without recording a considerable addition to my vocabulary and added colour to my education.

Needless to say the dray had to be unloaded and shoulders put to the wheels before it was extricated and reloaded. And all through the homeward trek, Mr Jones reinforced the day's lessons in a sequence of simmering undertones, like the after-shocks from a major earthquake.

Perhaps the most unpopular, and certainly the most undignified job on the farm side was the sanitary cart operators. The horse did the easy bit by pulling the flat-topped cart around the village and so frequently did it do its plodding that the complete outfit could have been registered as an automatic one-horse-powered dunny cart. The unpleasantries took the efforts of two boys. Working as a pair, they collected the used pans and left behind a nice, clean, freshly tarred empty.

Situated next to the engine-room, the timber yard was constantly employed in supplying firewood to the cook-houses, staff cottages and the girls' cottages. A stockpile of bush logs was being continually fed into the high-powered circular saw that was belt-driven straight from the engine room. An experienced man in Mr McCormick had been doing the saw work for years, and always had a team of boys under his direction, feeding logs to him and throwing the cut blocks onto a pile which another gang split into firewood. Once again the distribution was done by horse and cart and provided a permanent job for two boys.

Around behind the woodyard was the laundry, where a big team of girls worked under the supervision of Mr and Mrs A.E. Young. Thousands of items were laundered each week by these girls, dressed in their starched white pinafores and caps and handling huge cane baskets of washing to and from the clothes-lines.

Other facilities that required boys' labour were the poultry runs and the hospital, the former for collecting the eggs and cleaning the yards and bagging the manure, and the hospital for keeping the premises clean and polished.

SAILING BEFORE THE WIND

It was fairly certain that the Mandurah camp of 1937-38 would be my last as a Fairbridge boy. At fifteen years of age I could expect to be placed on a farm during the year. But this didn't necessarily mean the end of Mandurah for me. At the end of the State school holidays, usually in mid-February, the camp became available for use by holidaying Old Fairbridgians. Naturally, this privilege was greatly appreciated, not only for the enjoyment of an ideally situated holiday site, but also it provided an excellent opportunity for former school friends to renew acquaintances. It all depended, of course, on whether an employer would grant the annual two-week holiday break during the months of February or March.

The Fairbridge Society had bought a magnificent site on the estuary in Halls Head. And apart from a few private cottages on the foreshore, the camp enjoyed the double advantage of isolation in an almost idyllic wilderness position yet was only a short walk to either the town or the surf of the ocean rollers. This was the scene, then, to which we four senior boys brought our home-made sail determined to equal the adventures of Huck Finn up the Mandurah Estuary and on the broad waters of the Peel Inlet.

We were fortunate in having Mr Healey as camp principal because as Headmaster of the school, he had shared in our development over the years and showed his keenness to contribute further by giving us so much more freedom of action than had been previously permitted. No sooner had we made up our bunk beds, than an enthusiastic Reg Edwards had us hi-tailing it for the boat hirer's which was on the townside foreshore and in no time had clinched a favourable deal for the fortnight's hire of a solid four-metre clinker-built dinghy. When we beached our newly acquired status symbol in a tiny cove by our huts, I for one felt like a hundred pounds as we came ashore to the admiring reception of dozens of 'little kids'.

But there was no time for self-indulgence: no sooner had we made 'our' boat fast than Reg sent the rest of us for the boom, mast and sail. There was work to do.

I don't know where Reg got his knowledge from, but he knew exactly what had to be done. With the newly bought hanks of clothes-line, the sail was lashed to the boom, pulleys were tied in place, stays were positioned and halyards cut to length. Eventually our skipper gave the order to push off for our first trials, but with so much willing labour around the boat, we were spared this physical exertion. With Reg at the tiller, the boat floated free into the channel.

It was perfect timing. The late morning easterly breeze was dying, giving us near perfect conditions in which to make adjustments and familiarisation runs. The last thing Reg wanted was a strong wind to blow us onto the breakwater opposite while his crew were still novices. But in the light breeze he had us bobbing up and down, and moving this way and that, in a series of tacks. At the same time he taught us the language of sailing; the difference between port and starboard, bow and stern; we learnt to 'go about', and to watch out for the swinging boom, and we understood the meaning of jibing and luffing and pointing. We went into our midday meal with the swagger of seasoned sailors.

Overnight we became a team of experts, of adventurers. We had won a new-found status which gave us special privileges. From now on we could set sail immediately after the morning's inspection, with water and sandwiches stowed away enough to last the whole day. With Dick Darrington in the crew, we needed all the rations we could get. The fourth member was the lanky Peter Hassell whose natural ability to improvise would stand us in good stead if ever we became shipwrecked.

Every morning for days on end we tacked our way up the narrow channel of the estuary waving a casual salute to the hopefuls fishing beneath the bridge. Then, when we reached the broad expanse of the inlet, we tacked again to the shallows of the eastern shore before turning about for the run before the wind. This was a freedom never before experienced, never more enjoyable, never more exhilarating, being swept along with the splash and splurge of power from the wind-whipped sail while the four of us separately wrestled with our awakening emotions of manhood.

During a fortnight of growing maturity, the process involved converting learnt disciplines into instantaneous practicalities. And this period of transition was not all plain sailing. One particular foray into the Peel Inlet almost ended in disaster.

The usually predictable afternoon's sou'-westerly cooling breeze known locally as the Fremantle Doctor, arrived unexpectedly early, and swept in with a ferocity that caught us napping. Within a couple of minutes, a happy, harmonious crew was reduced to an argumentative rabble. In the confusion, discipline was discarded, orders were ignored, flying spray drenched us and we came perilously close to being swamped. Fighting the tiller to keep the bow into the waves, Reg quickly regained control with the sail being lowered and the oars manned. A few minutes later and he had us safely beached on a sandy island. With the danger over, our unity returned and we made ourselves a tent by draping the mainsail over the boom. Fortunately our sandwiches had been well stowed away so while the wind blew itself out, we took the opportunity to have a picnic.

It was incidents like this that formed the basis of life-long friendships. And although we were institutionalised adolescents deprived of parental love and affection, the very nature of our circumstance forged a substitute human bonding rarely found in limited sheltered family relationships. Restricted resources in no way lessened our enjoyment. Rather, it taught us to appreciate the true value of simplistic living by exploiting the full potential from every opportunity that arose. And opportunities came thickest during the comparative freedom of the Mandurah camping holidays. They have done so ever since Kingsley Fairbridge had marched his first handful of waifs the twenty-seven kilometres from the old farmhouse eight kilometres south of Pinjarra to enjoy the luxury of the unspoilt sleepy fishing village. That had been in 1912. Now, Mandurah is almost a city.

Life went along pretty smoothly at Scratton. After all, we were all about the same age, had spent several years at Fairbridge, and many of us belonged to the same organisations.

Although Mr Greenish was far from well, he treated us with dignity, fairness and above all with maturity. If he thought a lad had a problem, he would have a talk with him in the privacy of his cubicle often using his naval service in an analogous way.

'You need some direction in life Ramsbottom', he would say with a slight tilt of his head. 'If you don't have some guidance, some goal to aim for, you will be like a ship without a rudder, aimlessly going around in circles, never reaching your destination.' He spoke softly, earnestly, with great conviction. Furthermore we respected him for the service he had given his country.

Mrs Greenish was the nicest person I had met since leaving my mother. She always cooked something for the evening meal even though half a dozen boys would be cluttering up her kitchen. She just went on with her preparation talking and joking away as though they were her own boys. Scones were her speciality, and while they were cooking, she would let one of her boys skim the scalded cream from the saucepan of milk that simmered on the stove. When the scones were ready the boys scattered platefuls of them around the large area of combined dining tables. Mrs Greenish always insisted upon using table cloths which served to enhance the appearance of plates of bread, scones, jam and cream. The trouble was that there could be quite a wait for the late-comers to arrive, and the sight of all that food on display was tempting beyond measure. It was just my luck to get caught on the one occasion that I succumbed to the temptation and whipped a scone off the closest plate. But I wasn't quite quick enough. Hawk-eyed Reg Edwards had seen me, and in a flash half a dozen lads were giving me a hell of a time. And being guilty, there was nothing I could do but sit there and take it, until in a moment of inspiration I rose to my feet, and with an exaggerated gesture of penitence, I declared dramatically, 'Gentlemen, I'm extremely sorry, I beg your forgiveness'.

The effect was startling. Everybody roared with laughter; clearly I had been reinstated.

As part of our training, Mr Goulder the dairyman, frequently took carloads of us to a cross-section of farms throughout the surrounding districts, sometimes as part of a 'field-day', and other times just as a private visit by arrangement with the farmer. I remember one particular trip to an orange orchard near Harvey where, amongst other general orchard work, a demonstration of spraying was done. Then there was the usual session of questions and answers, and later, farmers formed small groups to exchange information and ideas. We boys undoubtedly learned something from these visits, but to us, any chance of a car ride was just like an outing; a day's jaunt away from the farm school.

On one occasion a carload of us started out from Fairbridge a little disappointed in the knowledge that we were going only as far as Pinjarra to watch an auctioneer's technique at the saleyards. But Mr Goulder was in a particularly happy mood as he drove steadily up the track commenting on the state of the farm's golf course that had been established in the previous two or three years.

'These fairways need cutting again, and I only had them done three weeks ago. The greens are coming along nicely though, if only the sheep could keep off 'em.' Then he'd lapse into a state of reflexion, whistling through his teeth the tune of his favourite hymn, *O Worship the Lord*.

A half hour of the auctioneer's chant was about as much as we boys could take, so one by one we sidled back for a more comfortable seat in the Essex which was one of about twenty cars parked either side of the South-West Highway. Although Mr Goulder had been careful to park his car on the correct side of the road facing back towards Fairbridge, some of the other car owners had shown less respect for the law by parking in any direction, indicating a certain leniency by country policemen. Not that that slight breach of the traffic code worried Ken McCullough as he sat in the driver's seat of the old Essex. The fifteen-year-old sandy-haired Scot was engaged in taking us all for a phantom spin through the south-west of the State, his hands throwing the steering wheel through imaginary tight curves and hairpin bends until he exhausted himself and sat back to rest.

It was during this period of recuperation that Ken spotted an uncharacteristic lapse in Mr Goulder's security. The key was in the ignition. For someone with such a fertile imagination, the temptation to try it gradually overpowered the reason of common sense, until he succumbed. If he had not held our interest during his make-believe excursion, he most certainly had it as his hand rested on the key.

With a flick of his wrist, the ignition started.

The immediate consequence of Ken's unfortunate lapse, was the incredible discovery that Mr Goulder had compounded his first error by leaving the car in gear. It says much for the efficiency of the maintenance that there was no hint of the engine stalling, no reluctancy at all on the part of the firing mechanism (a hesitancy that just might have alerted Ken to the potential danger of his movement). On the contrary, the slumbering Essex sprang to life like a bucking bronco, and without so much as an ounce of pressure on the accelerator, charged straight towards the next parked car.

What happened next was shameful by its decision, yet meticulous in its execution. Sensing that a catastrophe appeared imminent, the rest of us simply disappeared from the vehicle like a mass exodus of free-falling parachutists.

Considering that it was Ken's first driving lesson, without an instructor, he did astonishingly well. I had fully expected to hear an almighty crash about the same time as I landed, but nothing happened. For one frightening moment, I thought that I had damaged my hearing, so as quickly as I could recover I turned towards the action. What I saw filled me with instant admiration for the plucky lad.

Somehow he had managed to wrestle the Essex clear of the immediate danger, but was now headed towards a formidable line of parked cars on the opposite side of the road. With great presence of mind Ken once again wrenched the car away from the new peril. It was unfortunate then that he did what a number of novice drivers do: he over-corrected. Yet despite that, when he came back to his correct side of the road, some abberation must have confused his locating of the brake. Instead of using the pedal, he chose the front headlamp and mudguard of an incorrectly parked car. It was a double misfortune really, because another yard would have seen him in the clear with plenty of uncluttered space in which to bring the Essex to a more conventional stop. Then the voice from the saleyards that had been droning on for the best part of an hour, suddenly rose a couple of octaves which instinctively told Ken that he had hit the auctioneer's new car.

With the auctioneer temporarily disabled, there was a general movement towards the sound of tinkling glass as a last reluctant portion of headlamp hit the bitumen. By that time the auctioneer had recovered sufficiently to rush over to view the damage, and when he saw his spanking new car locking horns with an old Essex, his language somehow took on a familiar sound. All at once I recognised it as similar to Mr Jones's outburst a few weeks before, the only difference being a disparity in dialect.

On the other hand, Mr Goulder, showing remarkable restraint under most embarrassing circumstances, ushered us boys into the untangled Essex and headed for home, while the auctioneer's car made its undignified departure from the scene behind a tow truck.

In contrast to the morning's relaxed run into Pinjarra,

the return trip was an agony of tension. No whistling Mr Goulder now. I had a distinct feeling that he felt that the Lord had deserted him in his hour of need, and I could tell by the repetitive twitching of his upper lip and the deepening crimson patch on each cheekbone, that he was under considerable stress.

But my sympathies lay with Ken McCullough. In the grim silence, I couldn't help but reflect on the extraordinary adventure we'd just been through. While the rest of us had baled out of the car, he had kept his cool despite his lack of driving experience, and had managed to avoid two obstacles, hitting the third by the barest of margins. Extending my reflection further, I pondered on the outcome of the incident. If he had avoided everything, would he have kept going until he had run out of petrol? No, surely not; that was an insult to his intelligence. Rethinking again, I toyed with the idea that he chose to stop in the manner he did to spare us the ordeal of a long walk home. But then, why choose the auctioneer's brand new car? Surely something a little less ...

My ramblings jerked to a sudden stop along with Mr Goulder's exuberant application of the brake. We had arrived. No doubt a telephone call would have alerted the Principal in time to guarantee a reception in the office, the building which we were now entering.

When the few dents were knocked out of the tough old Essex and out of Ken McCulloch, we were soon back in Pinjarra attending the monthly Junior Farmers meetings. This organisation enjoyed great popularity at the time, particularly with us Fairbridge boys, because not only was it an introduction to meeting procedure, it gave us an opportunity to meet and mix with the local young men.

But after two or three meetings when interest waned slightly, it was discovered on visits to the outside lavatory that several of the local lads' bicycles were conveniently parked against the outside wall of the hall. With practically no access to push bikes in our lives before, this was the one simple thrill yet to be experienced. The chance could not be missed. Subsequently a roster system was organised among us designed to control the number of dunny visits to disciplined intervals. And much to our satisfaction and enjoyment, the system worked perfectly.

It was soon realised too, that burning up the streets of Pinjarra on a bike was a lot less dangerous than trying to negotiate them in the Essex. Not that Mr Goulder ever gave us another opportunity...

During 1938, a start was made on the Pinjarra golf course. The site was a few hundred metres out of town along the road to Mandurah. And it was heavily timbered, not so much with tall trees, but with thick patches of banksia, gum and sheoak, which was all given to Fairbridge. All we had to do was to cut the felled trees into logs of suitable lengths for Mr Nancarrow the Pinjarra carrier to cart to the farm school.

I was happy enough to be chosen as one of the three boys to work with the two hired hands to do the job. Every morning we'd collect our sandwiches from Mr Shugar while the men picked theirs up from the staff kitchen, and climb aboard the school van with our axes and crosscut saws. The driver then dropped us off at the job with the instruction that he would return at 4.00pm to pick us up. So far as I was concerned it was a day of freedom spent in the bush doing a job that I enjoyed. And there was no need for the men to supervise us; we did just as much work as they, although they usually let one of us knock off a bit earlier to boil the billy. Morning tea went with the job too, which was another pleasant little luxury. Mind you, it was well earned. It was continuous hard work, especially when loading Nancarrow's flat-topped truck. He had a method of stacking that never seemed to end.

But by the day's end I'd hop into the van pleasantly tired and look forward to a nice hot bath followed by a good tea and comfortable warm bed. I had a lot to be thankful for. I was certainly thankful for Mrs Greenish who was caring for us practically on her own. Her husband's condition had worsened, and he was now in hospital.

As the months went by, more and more of my friends left to make their way in the world. These were boys and girls whom I'd grown up with over the past five years; girls with whom I'd played tennis and danced; boys with whom I'd shared school, scouting, music, played cricket and football and more recently worked in a variety of jobs, learning new skills, enjoying new adventures.

Hardly a week went by without three or four leaving. Suddenly, a girl I'd known as a cut-kneed barefooted urchin turned up to breakfast in a smart dress, shoes and stockings and with make-up on. She was transformed overnight into an attractive young woman. The same with the boys. They'd come to breakfast suited, appearing a foot taller, now that they were out of short pants.

There had been differences, squabbles and fights over the years, the same as in any community, but generally the boys and girls at Fairbridge enjoyed a healthy relationship. After all, weren't we all members of one big family, brothers and sisters selected to share a new life together; a bond that would survive the childhood years and last throughout our lives as citizens of a growing nation?

In recent weeks I had farewelled Stan Trigg, Henry McCaughan, Reg Edwards, Dick Darrington, and several others. Once again the parting syndrome re-emerged to haunt me. Perhaps it was a reminder that the pendulum of life swings inexorably on in a repetitious cycle. Strangely, though, the loss of so many close mates failed to evoke in me any real depth of feeling. At the time there seemed to be no explanation for my indifference. Just an inexplicable void. In retrospect, perhaps I had left the core of my sensitivity drained on the moist earth of an English countryside railway station, where in one swift cruel moment of time my mother had been wrenched from me. And perhaps, subconsciously, ever since that moment, I had accepted that deep personal losses were to be an inevitable pattern of my life. But whatever the reason, I discovered that the rules of life sometimes did try to compensate, in part at least, for an apparent imbalance of justice.

Early in 1938 I was selected to respond to a request for

a penfriend from an English school girl of my own age. It was the beginning of a long friendship with a girl I never met, but who came into my life at a time when I most needed someone. Joan was well educated and wrote long, interesting and informative letters with a warmth that gave me a satisfying sense of wellbeing. At last, I felt that I had a genuine girl-friend.

But now that children were growing into adulthood and leaving the nest, the association didn't end. Far from it. That is why the Club House had been built at Fairbridge. Here was a club, a home to come back to, a place in which Old Fairbridgians could spend their holidays, to renew old friendships, to meet older Fairbridgians.

The Club House incorporated two separate accommodation wings protruding from each side of a central function area which also housed the manager and his wife. But it was the magnificent function room that held the key to the success of the place. A large kitchen at the rear was capable of catering for over two hundred guests seated in the main hall. Here it was that jarrah had been used to perfection in the construction of the vast floor, the strip panels in walls and ceilings, and the two folding partitions that effectively divided the central space into three rooms. A battery of ceiling fans made for pleasant summer conditions, while great granite open fireplaces at either end of the hall provided the feature attraction. It was around these roaring fires on wet winter nights that Old Fairbridgians set the rafters ringing with the melodies of favourite old songs brought from the 'old country', mixed with the ballads that told the story of their new land.

If Kingsley Fairbridge could have sat in on any one of these exhilarating gatherings, he would have been well rewarded with the evidence of a flourishing reality of his boyhood dream.

REVELATIONS

Five years of living in an Australian institution found me almost on the threshold of manhood. A few more months and I would be sixteen, working on some remote property far removed from the familiar facade of Fairbridge. But even with this approaching inevitability, I had not given it much thought. Experience had taught me to live for the day, and the day was pleasant enough spent in the Pinjarra bush with the ring of the axe and the swish, swish, swish of the saw. Seldom anything happened out of the ordinary; certainly nothing of note since Ken McCullough's daring drive. So when I arrived home one evening to find a letter from England on my bed in unrecognisable handwriting I opened it with a great deal of apprehension. But I had only to read the first few lines before I felt faint with shock.

I read the letter through the first time, mechanically, incapable of grasping the implication of its message. It was only after reading it for a second time that the true meaning emerged from the confusion that I felt. The one fact that seemed likely was that I now had a maternal mother. To say that I was totally unprepared would be the understatement of all time. It was like reading an unusual novel; a sequence of highly unlikely events leading the reader along to a premature unfinished ending. And the bizarre thing about it all was that the story was written by my own real mother, the woman who had given me life; and not only my life; for I had sisters — and who else?

It is difficult to recall my feelings at that moment. Perhaps turmoil could best describe them, although no single word could adequately explain the thoughts that fought for recognition in my mind. Ideas tumbled about in my brain like laundry in a tumble dryer. When it stopped spinning, a feeling of elation overwhelmed me as the realisation grew that I was no longer alone in the world; that at last I could say that magic word 'family'.

As I re-read the letter again and again, emotion registered in a number of different ways. In turn I experienced bewilderment, excitement, compassion and even a measure of disbelief.

Naturally, Mrs Greenish was delighted for me when I told her the incredible news my letter contained but advised me to discuss it with Canon Watson, a suggestion to which I readily agreed, and an appointment was made for the following day.

When the Canon had finished the reading, it surprised me to see the distinct lack of enthusiasm on his face. I would have thought that he, too, being a true Christian, would have been happy with the news. But when he talked it over with me, he sowed the seeds of doubt in my thinking. He put forward several questions for consideration: Why had my mother waited fifteen years before contacting me? Had she known about my leaving England over five years before, and if she hadn't, how did she discover my present address?

'And another thing', the Canon pointed out, 'you are about to go out into the world as a working man; you will be earning a wage. Be careful that your new-found mother is not after some financial assistance.' The Principal concluded by saying, 'By all means Ramsbottom, acknowledge your mother's letter, but my advice to you is be watchful in your future relationship with her. I sincerely hope that you will find happiness in the knowledge of your discovery, but do not rush into anything you may regret later.'

When I thought about Canon Watson's advice, I must admit there was a lot to think about, and now that the initial euphoria had subsided, amongst its replacement was a distinct feeling of disappointment that my mother had not sent me even one card in my whole life.

Nevertheless, I immediately wrote back to her Manchester address saying how excited I was to learn that after fifteen years of being an 'orphan', I could now boast having relations and would she reply soon to tell me about the rest of the story. In that first letter to her, I wrote a brief synopsis of my life story, in particular about my love for my foster parents who had given me such a wonderful childhood. I explained how I was on the threshold of a new life somewhere in the vastness of Western Australia, and that I would save up to come back to England some day and see her.

It was true, and only natural that I wanted some day to see her, but it was also true that if I ever returned to England my first call would be on the Nobeses, the people who had been my only parents.

But it soon became clear to me that it would be many years before I could afford such a trip. With Mr Greenish failing rapidly, Mrs Greenish broke the news to me that I had been found employment on a farm at Gnowangerup in the great southern part of the State. My employer was to be a Mr Monty House who ran a mixed farm of about a thousand acres, so I was to get good all-round farming experience. My starting wage was to be twelve shillings and sixpence per week, half of which was to be sent back to Fairbridge by the employer to be held in trust until I was twenty-one. I was to be provided with a complete new range of clothes which included underclothes, working gear, suit, overcoat and trilby hat. All I had to do with my half-wage was to maintain or buy new clothing, buy a bicycle with which to get into town to spend a weekly two shillings to see the picture show. And, of course, I was going to save up for my big trip.

Fortunately, my meals and accommodation were to be provided by Mr House, otherwise I would have been concerned about my solvency. But I still had a few weeks to wait, so that problem was put out of my mind. Of far more importance was the question of whether I would receive an answering letter from my mother before I left.

During the intervening few weeks I spent a lot of time thinking about the sequence of recent events that had overtaken me. Only a few months before I had been a forgotten orphan with only an occasional short letter from my foster mother to remind me that there existed at least one person who cared about me. Then, in the space of a couple of months, not only was I writing to an intelligent young lady penfriend, but out of the blue I suddenly discovered that I had a real live mother and a host of other relatives including sisters. But what concerned me was that there was no mention of a father. What of him? Where was this Mr Ramsbottom who had so gratuitously permitted me to suffer cruel inventive taunts from pitiless boys and mindless adults? And there were other questions...Was my mother genuinely concerned for me? How much had she suffered? How long did she keep me after I was born?

The answers came in a letter from my mother only a few days before I was due to leave Fairbridge. It arrived in a bulky square envelope. Mrs Greenish handed it to me with a sympathetic smile, her face pale and strained with the loss of her husband only two days before. Hurriedly I raced to my room, closed the door noisily behind me and tore open the envelope.

My Own Dear Son Jack,

I write these lines to you with great remorse and shame. To have to meet you and tell you face to face, I am afraid I could not bare to.

Well, I was born on 15th January 1894, rather delicate, had to be kept alive on the blood of raw meat for a long time (I believe). My mother says that I was the best baby she had and I grew up to be a nice child. Mother was very strict with us all until we grew to 14 years of age; trained us to clean and scrub and wash. Away to Sunday school from being tiny tots. As I grew to my early teens it was Chapel morning and evening — Sunday school afternoon. We are Baptist in religion. I was baptised when I was 18 years, then I became a Sunday teacher.

I was trained to be a waitress and was very happy at my work. Wages eight shillings and what tips were made; was a home girl -- tipped all my money up; that, we all had to do. Sixpence a week pocket money until 21 years of age.

At 20 I met my first boy — at 21 I had a lovely party. We were going to be engaged at his next leave, but he went to France and married a French girl. But he got let down — she could not bare him any children. That was his punishment, and me — a broken heart.

I must tell you that I have always been of a very nervous and afraid to go forward disposition, and still am. However, I was still working at this first class cafe when one afternoon two gentlemen walked in for tea and one of them knew me well, being the husband of the daughter of my parents' best friend. I was introduced.

They were Ministry of Supply officers — they were in uniform, the war was on. I got friendly with the one I was introduced to and he took me around. To me he was the perfect gentleman, until one evening he betrayed my trust, and I did not see him again until I found I was going to have his child. Until then I was a virgin.

He acknowledged it. He was of very wealthy stock and it was settled out of court for a sum of money, but to my surprise he had a wife who was awaiting a divorce. However, time went marching on — then Barbara arrived. Mother took over the entire charge of the baby, and the £250. Then I met another bitter sorrow. From church, they crossed me right off the membership. I was grieved indeed — so all the family stopped going.

Time went on and I was still working and looking after Barbara and having things rammed down my throat. Then one Saturday evening my parents brought some friends home for a musical evening — they were all members of a concert party. We had a lovely home, plenty of music and plenty of drink, though we were never allowed to touch anything. My parents' friend and her husband brought her brother along one evening, quite a nice smart man about my own age; he was an accountant and they were quite a nice family.

However we got friendly and he knew about me having Barbara and we started going around together. I found I got fond of him and a little later on I found I was going to have a child by this man, and his name was Harry Mills. Need I tell you that he had no honourable intentions towards me. He made Barbara the excuse and denied everything, so I just could not be bothered with him any more.

I had to leave home. I went to Ramsgate in Kent. I worked until as long as I could, as a waitress, then I went to hospital and there you, my Son was born — perfect and beautiful.

How I loved you!

I got well and I transferred to Manchester hospital, and then my parents had to claim me from there. I went home — went out to work to keep us both — got in touch with Harry Mills again to see if he was going to help maintain you — but frankly refused. My life was hell on earth at home so I packed up and with my son Jack, — you, we travelled back to the county where you were born — Kent. Being a holiday and seaside resort, I could only work the summer season. I had to take what digs I could find, that would look after you while I was working. It was a horrible place for both of us to be living in.

Then I met a man there. It was my day off duty. I had taken you down to the beach and I was feeling down in the dumps and homesick. However, I kept seeing this man when I was at liberty, and told him that you were my baby — and about Barbara. When he decided to marry me I thought it might be one way out (to my sorrow). Well we came back to Manchester and went to my parents and were married from there, and lived there.

If ever there was a human beast — he was it. Never, in all my experience have I ever met such a man. Then, after a few months, one morning I came down and found that a solid marble clock was missing from the dining room. I got my mother out of bed and we looked around and found that other articles had gone. We went to his place of work, and found that they did not know such a man. Then we went to the police and got a warrant for his arrest. I did not have a photograph of him but the description I gave the police of him tallied with someone they were after from other parts of the country. But he was never found, and I have never seen or heard of him from the day he walked out on me.

But the worst had happened — I was left expecting a baby. That was Norah — our Norah Buckthorpe.

Then I had to go to work again until baby was born, then I got well again and had to start working once more. I got a foster-mother for you on conditions that I could see you every night and have you to myself on weekends. You were only there about three weeks when I discovered that the master of the house beat you and put you in the cellar — they only wanted the money for drink. So one night, I watched and waited for them going out. Then I brought you away. I had got the place from the Ministry of Health. They were registered as foster parents. I got them taken off the Register. However, I had a hell of a life at home.

So my mother got busy among her friends and with influence, got you in Dr Barnardo's, and Norah at Mrs Mathews at Blackburn. But believe me, my hands were forced; I had not a say in the matter, and what my mother did she thought it the best — that you would get an education.

Then I became the slave and drudge of the house,

and going out to work, tipping my money up and drudging at home after a days work. But I still stuck to my parents, and have done till recently.

So now my Dear Son, I have opened my soul and mind to you, but please do not think I have been all bad. No — I never went dancing or drinking or cursing. My only recreation was swimming and life-saving. But you can rest content that, You, Norah and Barbara are pure — free from all complaint and disease; you were never tried to be got rid of. I am proud of you my dear, and not ashamed of you. It's myself I am ashamed of for putting too much trust in people. But even today, I am just the same disposition, ready and willing to help anyone — any person in distress or trouble. I have tried to redeem my sins by trying to do what I can for others. The old saying is 'Reward is in Heaven' — well I trust so. There will be peace at least, and I don't care when that time comes. When God is ready to take me — I am ready.

So now my Dear Son, have no fear about your birthright, but I am extremely sorry for all the anxiety I have caused. I ask you my Dear, to forgive me. If you are ever in any trouble and you just have enough to get over to me, come to me. I shall be waiting with open arms. Darling, if only I could express myself plainly I am sure you would not judge me so.

I want to ask you my Son for one photograph of yourself, just in case you decide to disown your Mother. If so, please answer this and tell me so — then I shall understand.

For now, I will say cheerio and God bless you, ever and ever. There is more I will tell you next time if there ever is one,

Your Sorrowing Mother xxxxx
(I Love You all)

On the back of the first page was a postscript.

I guess you think I had forgotten you, but I admit
this is the most dreadful job I have ever had to do
because, I know that I have to hurt you, my own
Son.

Long before I came to the end of the tension-packed pages,
tears distorted my vision and trickled down my cheeks. I
felt only sadness — deep and overwhelming compassion for
the woman who had endured so much. And the woman who
had struggled and fought her way through a wretched life,
had relived it all in the humility of her confession, was my
mother.

It was so bewildering, unbelievable almost. If so tragic
a sequence of events had appeared in a novel, they would
have been read with scepticism. But what I had just read
was true. It had to be the truth; no woman would ever
condemn herself so courageously if it were otherwise.

Right there and then I vowed I would go to her as soon
as I saved the fare even though it seemed an impossibility
on the paltry wage I would be earning. In the meantime,
I would write to reassure her of my gratitude for her
frankness and honesty, and that I would never entertain
the thought of disowning the woman who had given me life.
I would let her know that although I had suffered heart-
wrenching separations from loved ones in the past, time
had helped heal the scars, and that there had been so much
to be thankful for in my life.

I would tell her I was well and strong; that I had learnt
new skills, new sports; that I could swim and save life, and
that in a few days I would be leaving behind my boyhood,
donning long pants and going out into the world as a young
man to be a farmer.

I pondered on her latest name of Mrs Jones that had
been revealed in her first letter. She had said nothing of
her husband. I hoped that now, at last, she had found
happiness in marriage and enjoyment in life.

Slipping the letter back into the envelope, I placed it in
the far corner of my desk drawer. No one must see it, not
even Mrs Greenish. The pain behind the story would be

Jack Ramsbottom's mother, in a photograph she sent to him in 1954.

meaningless to other people. Better to keep it between mother and son.

The 23 September 1938 was a milestone in my life. It was the day my childhood finished. It was my turn to leave Fairbridge. Exactly five years and four months before I had chugged into the village on the back of an old lorry a bewildered and unhappy little boy. I would never forget the turbulence of that day. Yet over the past five years, not only had I survived that initial shock, I had weathered the initiation into a vastly different environment, graduating through the tough disciplined ranks of the barefooted urchin brigade right up into the senior boy's status. Today was the day I would shed my short pants to become a man. At any rate, I was dressed the part.

Self-conscious in my neat blue suit and new shoes, I entered the main dining hall and strode to my place at the long central table for the last time. For over twenty years several hundred old girls and boys had gone before me, each one the centre of attention. Knowing now that all eyes would be upon me, I suddenly became aware of a new-found esteem; a realisation that a whole new life lay ahead of me, that destiny was sweeping me into the uncertainties of the future.

The order to stand and say Grace brought me back to earth, and as I settled into my place on the form to help pass the porridge plates along the table, I wondered if it would be the last time I would sit down to a breakfast of bread with dripping and jam. Little did I suspect that in the not too distant future, I would spend many sleepless nights craving for just one mouthful of the food I was sick of eating that morning.

After breakfast there was time enough for me to take one last stroll along the top road to the church. It was an opportune moment to let my gaze wander towards the white painted railings that enclosed the grave of Kingsley Fairbridge, the man who had made it all possible for me and thousands of other British foundlings to be given the chance of a quality of life that most certainly would not have been available in the orphanages of Britain. Here at

1/10/38

KINGSLEY FAIRBRIDGE FARM SCHOOL

NAME _Ramsbottom_

........./..Case with straps		13 —
........./..Rug		13 6
........./..Best Suit	2	— —
......../..Best Shirt		3 9
........./..Best Boots		9 6
........./..Working Boots _& laces_		15 1
......2..Working Trousers @ 6/8		13 4
......2..Working shirts @ 5/6		11 —
......../..White shirt		3 6
......2..Pairs Pyjamas @ 5/6		11 —
......2..Blue Singlets @ 1/4		2 8
......../..White Vests		1 6
........./..Jerseys		5 —
......../..Felt Hat		6 —
........./..Straw Hat		1 9
........./..Pair Braces		1 8
......../..Leather Belt		1 8
......../..Ties		1 7
......5..Handkerchiefs		1 2
......3..Pairs Socks		3 10
..../..½..Towels		5 -
......../..Toothbrush		10
......../..Toothpaste		1 —
......./..Writing Pad & Envelopes		1 2
......./..Pen & Bottle Ink		4
......./..Cake Soap, Studs & Links 7½		1 —
......./..Oil Skin Coat _Overcoat_ 3	1	4 9
Hairbrush, Clothes Brush & Nail Brush.		3 9
Hussif		2 -
Boot Polish		5
	10	1 9

THIS OUTFIT IS THE GIFT OF THE
FAIRBRIDGE FARM SCHOOL, given when
you proceed to your first employment.

A copy of the list of items given to Fairbridgians upon leaving
the institution.

Fairbridge, we were an ever-expanding family of brothers and sisters sharing a unique experience that would survive for as long as children of Old Fairbridgians lived.

Lifting my gaze beyond the Founder's grave to the giant granite outcrops of the Darling Ranges, I was reminded of how their rugged beauty differed so much from the softer lines of the Cotswolds. Inevitably, my thoughts drifted back to the carefree days spent in exploring the woods around Eastcombe together with the special charm of the Toadsmoor Valley. I pictured the family group climbing the winding secluded track through the hills and on into Stroud. The happiness of those early childhood years enveloped me in a flood of nostalgia until the conflict of competing loyalties suddenly thrust itself upon me.

Now there was my new-found family to think about. Again, doubts crept in, new questions surfaced. What had my real mother said? 'There is more to tell you next time.' Had there not been enough last time? Just how much more could there be? She had sought, and I had given her my assurance and understanding. The only exception had been the question of my name. For the life of me, I couldn't understand why I hadn't been given my father's name of Mills. My mother would have done me a big favour if she had done that instead of saddling me with the family name of Ramsbottom. That name might be familiar enough around Manchester, but to wear it through years of institutional life is a fate no child should suffer.

No other thought could have brought me back more quickly to the realities of the moment. It was only after a lengthy period of familiarity that the taunts and insults dried up. Now that I was leaving my friends to meet strangers in the outside world, I knew I'd have to go through it all over again.

With a wry smirk, I headed back towards Scratton and the waiting school vehicle. In a sudden burst of angry frustration, I aimed a savage kick at a cluster of dandelions sending the severed heads flying. At the same time I choked out a frustrated warning: 'Look out Australia, here comes that little Pommy bastard Jackie Ramsarse.'

The Ramsbottom family. From left, back row – Grandfather and Grandmother Ramsbottom, and Jack Ramsbottom's Aunt Phylis and Uncle Reg; centre – Aunt Muriel; front – Jack Ramsbottom's sister, Barbara and her husband Alf.

EPILOGUE

Over the past few years many Old Fairbridgians have returned to the United Kingdom, often at the request of their own children wishing to compile a family tree, to meet recently discovered family members. Not all these visits have met with success. A few have resulted in bitter disappointment, time being the main barrier in effecting a reconciliation. Others have fared better for a while, meeting with initial goodwill, only to find the relationship sours when the parties realise they have little in common. But many reunions have been successful. Quite often we read stories of a brother and sister, after being separated in childhood, rediscovering each other in another Commonwealth country in their retirement years. Some Old Fairbridgians have recently traced previously unknown family members only to be welcomed on arrival by a whole tribe of relatives, resulting in long-lasting happiness.

Apart from meeting my my mother's brother, Harold Ramsbottom and his family during my wartime training near Adelaide in 1941, my own story of family reunion began on my first trip back to the Old Country in 1976. Yet, on that occasion, my first consideration was the return to the scene of my greatest happiness. In all my forty-three years of absence, particularly through five years of war, three and a half of it which were spent in a Japanese prisoner-of-war camp, there was never a homecoming of greater emotion than my return to Bismore and Eastcombe. The love of a woman added the vital ingredient. My wife, Ronda, was with me to share my happiness.

But all too soon we had to move on. Ronda's relatives lived in the north of Scotland and we were anxious to see them before winter set in. I would be meeting them for the first time, so this whole trip was fast turning into a journey of discovery.

As we drove back out of Scotland into England's northwest, I talked over with Ronda the facts of my earlier brief contact with my mother and two half-sisters. The war years, of course, put an end to our recently established relationship, but with my release from a Japanese prisoner-of-war camp, I quickly contacted them and regular correspondence resumed. However after five or six years our letters grew less frequent until they ceased altogether. Now I didn't even have their addresses. All I could remember was that my mother (who, I suspected, had probably passed away by this time) and elder sister, Barbara, had lived in Manchester while Norah and her family had been in Blackburn. As Blackburn was the smaller of the two, we decided that we'd have a far better chance of locating Norah. But with a gap of twenty-five years since our last letters, I wasn't too optimistic about the outcome.

Nevertheless, as we took the road to Blackburn, I couldn't help but find the feeling of apprehension gradually churn into a distinct simmer of excitement the closer we drew to our destination. At that stage I had no idea what I would do when we did arrive

We were listening to a program from the BBC, when the presenter identified its source as Radio Blackburn. And suddenly the solution came to me. What better method of starting our search than soliciting the help of the BBC

The receptionist at the BBC office listened politely as I briefly explained my purpose. My spirits rose as a growing interest turned to enthusiasm, and then she ushered us into the office of a journalist.

Mike Marsh put me immediately at ease. After a friendly greeting he busied himself with a recording machine explaining the need to tape our conversation for possible broadcasting during his afternoon session. Then with skillful questioning he drew from me the pertinent facts of my life's circumstances that brought me from Australia to Blackburn at the age of fifty-three, in the hope of finding a sister whom I had never met.

Three-quarters of an hour later Mike farewelled us at the front office with the assurance that he would edit and play the tape that afternoon, asking any listener who may have information of my sister Norah Barnes to contact the station. He suggested we call back to reception at five pm where we could collect any waiting messages.

It was a day that stays in the memory. Apart from the agony of the long wait for news, winter had arrived with a vengeance, carpeting the streets of Blackburn with a layer of ice that threatened potential disaster with every careful step.

The receptionist greeted us when we returned with the news that Norah's ex-husband had heard the broadcast and had left her address with the station.

It was almost unbelievable. To have achieved success within a few hours of arriving in town was beyond my fondest expectation. For a few moments I stood stunned, my eyes rivetted on the piece of paper the smiling receptionist held out for me. When I eventually found my voice to thank her profusely, she helped us out further by explaining the way to Norah's place. Once again I thanked the receptionist, and we made our excited exit with her shouted good wishes following us.

But when the first wave of excitement subsided a little, we realised it might be too much of a shock for Norah to find two strangers arriving on her doorstep on a bleak winter's night, so we decided to wait until the morning. Being a Saturday we figured, too, we'd have a better chance of finding her home.

When we did eventually muster the courage to operate her doorknocker, I grasped the knob, gave three loud raps, took a pace back, and waited. After several seconds there was a sound of a turning key before the door opened slowly. I looked at the dressing-gowned woman standing inquisitively in the doorway, and instinctively knew that for the first time in my life I was staring at my sister.

It was obvious she hadn't been out of bed very long and all I could think of was that perhaps Ronda and I should not have called so early. But already a look of suspicion clouded her face and I knew I'd have to explain who we were, only I'd forgotten how I'd planned to introduce ourselves. In the end I suddenly blurted out, 'Norah, I'm your brother Jack from Australia.'

Norah stood there eyeing me over for a long time, obviously struggling to come to terms with this astounding start to her day. For one brief moment I thought she might slam the door in my face. But when she spoke, it came in the broadest of Lancastrian accents. 'Oh! Well ... you'd better come in then.'

In the years that followed, whenever we met Norah never tired of reminding us of that memorable morning when she thought Ronda and I were trying to put over some sort of confidence job. Now, having made the breakthrough, we spent the next week meeting Norah's complete family of three sons and two daughters with their spouses and offspring. The exception was her youngest son, Stephen, who was still at school. All of a sudden Ronda and I were overwhelmed by a host of ready-made family members. We even let the local newspaper in on the event and they responded by sending out a reporter. The following day Norah and I appeared in the paper happily toasting our historic meeting.

But I still had one more objective in mind; to find my elder sister, Barbara. Norah had confirmed that my mother had in fact passed away, as I had suspected.

Unfortunately Norah and Barbara had drifted apart over the years. Talk about a fragmented family! Seven years had passed since their last letters to each other. We were left with no alternative but to drive to Barbara's last known address in Manchester and hope for the best.

As we had half expected, our run of good fortune in finding Norah seemed to desert us in our early enquiries. No one by the name of Barbara Jarrat lived at the address we had. There was nothing for it but to canvass the whole street. But the street was a long one and we spent a couple of hours doorknocking without success. It was all very discouraging and we had just about resigned ourselves to failure when our luck changed.

With only a handful of houses left to call on, a kindly middle-aged woman opened her door to us with some encouraging information. She knew where Barbara's daughter-in-law lived. She not only helped us find the vital phone number, but insisted that we ring immediately. After a hurried consultation it was decided to let Norah do the talking, so she dialled the number while the rest of us held our breath. A minute later we had the address we were after. Barbara lived in Cleveleys.

But a further week passed before we made the link-up. Cleveleys is a small west coast town a few miles north of Blackpool, so it was a good two hours' drive from Blackburn. It was an enjoyable trip, full of apprehension and pleasant anticipation, and I had little difficulty in finding Barbara's house.

That December Sunday in 1976 turned out to be a day of significant discovery for me. For not only did I find my sister Barbara, but I met what I thought to be my only surviving aunt, Auntie Phyllis, and her two daughters, Dorothy and Renee. It was certainly an historic occasion. At fifty-three years of age, I had at last been reunited with my closest living blood relations. Emotion ran a banker that day. My mother had had a brother and four sisters and I was grateful to have been able to at least meet two of them, Phyllis and Harold.

From that memorable week, I kept in touch with them all, making sure I visited them on several subsequent trips back to the UK. I had left it far too late to see my mother, and it was just as well we made that first trip when we did, as just three years later, while I was in the early stages of making plans to bring Barbara out to Western Australia,

Barbara, Jack and Norah, reunited.

news came through that she had died suddenly of a heart attack. She was only sixty-one years of age. I was deeply saddened by her loss.

Barbara's death served to strengthen my resolve to give Norah a chance to see Fairbridge Farm, the school that had been my home for over five years in the '30s, and had so fortuitously more than adequately prepared me for the rigours of my life that lay ahead.

She came in 1983, and loved it so much she didn't want to go home. The day she arrived back in Blackburn, she started saving for a return visit. But it was a trip she was destined never to make. By a cruel twist of fate, a few days before her scheduled flight out she, too, had a heart attack and lingered only a couple of days. Then only a few months later, my cousin Dorothy wrote with the news that her mother, my Auntie Phyllis, had passed away. I was losing my newly found family all too quickly.

In 1988 I returned yet again to England, mainly to seek information from my personal file at Barnardos for use in writing my autobiography. During my visit, as always, I spent some time visiting friends around Eastcombe where I had spent my early childhood.

And quite naturally, after having spent so much effort in locating my Lancashire relatives, I always reserved a few days for my Blackburn tribe, after which I'd pop over to Fleetwood where Dorothy was living. As she was now on her own, I stayed to have lunch with her, and during the meal she came out with some astonishing information. I had told her that having lost both my sisters and Auntie Phyllis, I now felt she was just like another sister to me. She replied quite matter-of -factly. 'But of course, you do have another auntie still alive. Your mother's sister, Muriel, is living down in Cheadle, just south of Manchester.'

This startling piece of news left me speechless for quite some time. Several questions were racing through my mind. Why had she not spoken of Auntie Muriel before? Does she not realise the importance I attach to my search for my family? Was there friction amongst branches of the family? Could my recent resurrection have brought embarrassment to some of them? Whatever the reason, whatever the consequences, I knew I couldn't return to Australia without meeting this newly discovered auntie.

When I eventually found my voice, I managed to control my concern, not wishing to cause Dorothy unnecessary distress. But I was soon to find that one discovery inevitably led to others. In answer to my query as to how I could contact my new auntie, Dorothy gave me the phone number of Muriel's eldest daughter Jean, who lived nearby. Because Jean and her husband worked, I had to wait until the evening to contact them. Introductions and explanations accompanied my phone call of course, but Jean seemed genuinely delighted to hear from me and explained how to get to her mother's place.

Auntie Muriel welcomed me from her wheelchair, arthritis having reduced her to this method of mobility. She talked about my mother guardedly, mentioning her qualities of kindness and gentleness, attributes that had contributed to many of her difficulties. I liked Muriel. She was mentally bright and had a ready wit. I was sorry I could not stay longer with her. But I was fortunate enough to be invited to spend the night at Jean and David's home. It was the start of a whole new chain of events.

For four years we kept in touch hoping that one day in the not too distant future the fragmented Ramsbottom clan would all get together in one grand family reunion. The opportunity came when Ronda and I decided to return to the UK for a reunion stemming from my wartime association with the crew of the British aircraft carrier H.M.S. *Formidable.* She had brought twelve hundred surviving prisoners of war from Japanese hands back home to Australia.

Once Jean and David received our news they set to work on our master plan. So successful were they in their telephone campaign that they found it necessary to hire a hall for the occasion.

It all came to fruition on the night of the 26 September 1992. Ronda and I walked into the Bramhall Leisure Centre to find over seventy members of the Ramsbottom family waiting to welcome us. Cousins came from all over the north of England. Two carloads drove down from Blackburn, one drove up from Milton Keynes. Not every relative attended of course. Dorothy wasn't well enough to make the trip, and some were overseas. Sadly, Auntie Muriel had passed on. Yet there was no denying it was a memorable occasion.

Yet, strangely perhaps, throughout the entire night, I sensed no special feelings of emotion. The effort of trying to remember to put names to so many new faces taxed my ailing memory and left me with little time for contemplation. It was in the days that followed, after viewing a film

John Lane and some of his extended family at the Ramsbottom reunion.

David made of the occasion and looking through the album of family groups compiled by Jean, that initiated quiet periods of reflection.

I had accomplished what so many Old Fairbridgians had set out to do in their retirement years — to trace their roots in the Old Country, seeking knowledge of the people responsible for their very existence in order to pass on to their offspring the origins of their birthright.

Yet despite my apparent success, I found that at seventy years of age, the absence of a childhood relationship with any of them had left me with a distinct feeling of remoteness — of a void in my subconscious like a deep well which yields no water. By comparison, I find that my frequent thoughts of Bismore and Eastcombe are synonymous with one of life's most precious gifts — the gift of love.

Eastcombe village looked almost deserted. Occasionally a lone figure or two sauntered along the main street to disappear into the Lamb Inn or on down the hillside. Somewhere overhead, lost in the clear blue sky of a perfect spring day, a busy skylark trilled a lively overture at the promise of an early summer.

But despite the lofty performance, it failed to lift the depressing mantle of neglect that enveloped the burial ground. Most of the graves lay abandoned beneath years of uncut grass. Grey and melancholy headstones stood in irregular formations like stragglers from a defeated army, frozen in time. Many inscriptions were indecipherable, the wording barely visible beneath the mossy growth.

The exception was an immaculately kept grave a few paces inside the gate. Rising from its bed of marble chips, a tall engraved headstone clearly identified it as that of my old pastor, 'The Reverend S.G. Johnson M.M. the Baptist Minister of Eastcombe from 1925 to 1953.' The Military Medal had been won for bravery in World War I.

The spring of 1982 was not my first trip back to Eastcombe. I made my first nostalgic return to an old 'stomping ground' in the autumn of 1976, forty-three years after my traumatic parting from the only family I had ever known. It had been a visit of conflicting emotions; happiness at seeing again so many familiar places, yet, at the same time, a nagging feeling of guilt that I had failed to come back in the lifetime of my foster mother and father.

Even after all these years a few old acquaintances still lived in the village. Most astonishing of all was the discovery that Mrs Johnson, the late Reverend's widow, and Miss Rogers, an old schoolteacher, still survived. I unearthed, too, a sprinkling of my former football heroes, including Eastcombe's brilliant goalie Lionel Fawkes. When he presented me with a photographic memento of the team's most successful 1931-32 season, I was deeply moved.

I had long since discarded the name of Ramsbottom, not being particularly endeared to it. There was also the incentive to spare my own children from embarrassment.

Naturally, this name change led to a spate of explanations as I caught up with these old villagers.

The village as I had known it had not changed much. Certainly it had expanded, with the resultant loss of open space, and despite the attempt to give the new houses the distinctive dignity of the original Cotswold stone cottages, the result was a little disappointing. They all looked so obviously new. Perhaps time would be the blender.

But the heart of Eastcombe had remained pleasantly preserved. The untouched beauty of the scattered houses, my old school, the quadruple-chimneyed Manse and the chapel with it's belltower and clock were just as I had remembered them, although the clock had long since stopped. The Lamb Inn with its quaintly smiling signboard lamb still gazed longingly at the grass on the village green. How small that triangular patch of turf had become. Old eyes have a habit of shrinking childhood vistas, while the brain seems to act in reverse. Nostalgic recollections of the many post-school encounters on this pocket battleship-sized sportsground had come flooding back. Wry smiles creased my tanned face at the memory of those abandoned football matches when all hands had fought to retrieve flying sheets of newspaper.

But my most exciting moment came when I paused at a point halfway down Bismore Hill from where I had had my first view of Nobes' cottage. Strangely enough, it was not so much the house that took my attention, but rather the copse of beech trees immediately behind it. In my childhood I had spent many happy hours climbing into the low branches of those young trees. Now they were a towering backdrop of stately trunks topped with masses of bare branches that seemed almost to reach the sky.

This had the effect of making 'our' house look even smaller than it was. But it looked much the same as I had remembered it, tucked snugly into the hill with the trees on the high side almost hiding one pair of chimney pots. The two dormer windows protruding from the slate grey roof and the matching front porch were still intact. After all those years the only change that I could see had been the installation of a skylight high in the roof.

But below the cottage, the once unspoilt beauty of the meadow had been polluted by an unsightly row of electric light poles. In my view, the hamlet of Bismore had paid dearly for the price of progress.

Later that day I had searched in vain for the graves of my foster parents and Auntie Flo. Many years of neglect had made my task almost hopeless. It had left me disappointed and a little angry that no one had taken the trouble to at least keep the burial sites recognisable. That was why I had made a silent promise that someday I would do something about it. Their years of unselfishness and compassion in providing love and shelter to so many foundling children should never be forgotten.

Then, in 1982, I returned to keep my promise. This time I discovered that Arthur Johnson still lived in the village and had kept an association with the chapel. He had grown from the baby I had known into a man as gentle and kind as his father. He also had his father's slight build and swarthy, sharp features. Five minutes with Arthur and I knew that I had come to the right man. After a quick search of the chapel records he took me straight to the lost graves. Then a few more minutes spent in clearing away the long grass and ivy, uncovered an identifying marker bearing the initials S.N. (Samuel Nobes). The adjoining grave was Auntie Flo's.

I had previously discussed with a stonemason in Stroud just what I wanted. Now that I was able to confirm the order, he gave it first priority. He understood that my return flight to Australia was less than a fortnight away. A few days later he told me it was finished. He would deliver and install it on the Saturday, about four o'clock.

When the afternoon eventually arrived, I drove up to Eastcombe well before the promised time of delivery. This was one appointment I was making sure I didn't miss. How fortunate too, I thought, that the light was good for taking pictures. I sat on the perimeter wall armed with my cameras, and with only the tireless skylark for company, I waited.

Right on time, the stonemason's covered van drove slowly along the main street and stopped just past the cemetery gates. Two men climbed from the van. I started filming.

The load was heavy. The headstone looked weighty enough, but to keep it well anchored in the ground, a bulky concrete block had been fixed to its base. For the fifty-metre carry to the gravesite, the stonemason and his assistant used a wire cradle suspended from a long pole. Then, taking the load on their shoulders, they shuffled their way to the grave. Ten minutes later the stone was in position, and after making sure I was satisfied with the placement, they walked quietly back to the van. I was alone by the graveside.

Now, even the skylark seemed to have sensed the poignancy of the moment and hushed its voice, leaving me to meditate in silence. I was so engrossed in my retrospection that I had no idea that two men had entered the cemetery and were coming my way. My attention was rivetted to the neatly engraved inscription. Slowly and deliberately I read aloud the simple words:

IN
MEMORY OF
ROSA AND SAM NOBES
WHOSE LOVE AND KINDNESS GAVE
ME A WONDERFUL CHILDHOOD
THEIR LOVING 'SON' JACK

It was only when I finished that I became aware that I had company. Instinctively turning to face them, a warm feeling went through me as I recognised the shorter of the two as Arthur Johnson. After all his help, I was delighted he had come to share this moment with me. But I had no idea who his tall bulky companion was.

Answering my enquiring look, Arthur said softly, 'I thought you'd like to have a special guest at this family reunion Jack. Do you remember your favourite foster brother ... George Brown?'

In writing this Epilogue to my Fairbridge memoirs, I place myself unreservedly among the majority of Old Fairbridgians who remain forever grateful for having been given the opportunity to make a meaningful contribution to the development of this great country. Out of a total of around three thousand children that went through the system, some five hundred and fifty old boys and girls gave up to five years service to their new country during World War II. Sadly, fifty-five Old Fairbridgians were killed in action or died while prisoners of war.

During our formative years at the Farm School and again as young fledgling men and women, we spread our wings over most parts of this vast State of Western Australia, we were ever mindful of the many sacrifices made on our behalf by our founder Kingsley Fairbridge during his tragically short life. The Principal advised us to stick to our jobs even if we found it rough going, at least until the half-yearly visit of the after-care officer gave us the chance to talk things over. It was also instilled in us to always give of our best and at all times do nothing to dishonour the good name of Fairbridge. Farmers were going through difficult times so we should remember that the training we had been given had been specially designed to prepare us for the tough times ahead.

How right he was!

Conditions at Fairbridge were almost palatial by comparison to the living quarters of my first job.

I shared a two-roomed stone cottage with another man, a teamster from Albany. Our sleeping arrangements were very basic. A couple of tattered blankets covered a slim fibre mattress on each iron bedstead. A sizeable gap between the floorboards and the walls provided an ideal breeding ground for hordes of fleas. A wooden plank stretched across two kerosene cases was our only furniture. The amenities comprised a small enamel bowl, an oval-shaped tin tub and a four- gallon kerosene tin that served as a bucket. On Sundays, a fireplace in the other room enabled us to heat water for a bath and do our washing. The rest of the week we washed in the bowl alongside a thousand-gallon water tank at one end of the cottage. There was no toilet for our use. We had to walk a hundred yards to the back of the pigsty behind the stables. At least we had privacy there, apart from the inquisitive grunts from the neighbouring occupants.

A few weeks after my arrival the teamster left, and I was given his job.

Although I wasn't particularly keen on farming (my interests leaning towards the arts), the skills I had learnt at Fairbridge certainly helped me through the two and a half years I spent at Mr House's farm. In fact, in that short time my wages had doubled, going from twelve shillings and sixpence a week to twenty-five shillings. I had progressed from being just a farm labourer to the responsible position of teamster in control of ten magnificent horses.

In recent years, when access to our personal files was introduced, I was pleasantly surprised to read that Mr House rewarded my efforts with the comment, 'Jack is doing a man's work so I'm paying him a man's wage.' And all that at the age of seventeen.

But now the world was at war and young Australians everywhere were joining up.

Shortly after my eighteenth birthday I said farewell to Mr and Mrs House, my ten horses and Larry the slobbering bulldog, and made for Perth. Then, armed with my trombone for which Fairbridge had advanced the money, I presented myself at the Francis Street Barracks, declared myself to be twenty-one, and gained immediate acceptance into the Australian Army.

It was the start of a new career.

The story of my five years' wartime experiences is told in my book *Summer Will Come Again*. You may justifiably think that I returned from spending three and a half years in a Japanese prisoner-of-war camp a wiser man. However, shortly after I took my discharge from the army, I made the biggest mistake of my life.

I married the first attractive girl who appeared to take an interest in me and, more importantly, didn't object to sharing my uncommon name.

By this time I had resumed writing to my natural mother and also to two recently discovered half-sisters. But over the following five years my letters gradually faded the further my marriage deteriorated. It was during this period too, that I changed my name by deed poll. By 1952 both my marriage and contact with my family had ended.

My other big postwar mistake was my failure to contact my foster parents.

Try as I might, I cannot give any reason for this abysmal behaviour. A possible excuse is that my confused state of mind during this period of my life just couldn't cope with the stress. Whatever the cause, this lack of action on my part remains one of my deepest regrets.

Perhaps destiny, fate, or whatever it's called, has attempted to square the ledger somewhat by arranging a totally unexpected reunion with my foster sister, Florence Taylor. She is the Florence Bottomley mentioned in the first chapter who used to take me out with her whenever she visited 'our Mum'. After a parting of sixty-three years I can tell you that emotions erupted when we embraced in a meeting too consuming for words.

Florence, now a widow, lives comfortably in a group of self-contained retirement units in the town of Odiham, Hamphire. I shared five days of spiritual happiness with Flo and met many of her family. Even though we have no blood ties, it was as though I had at last come home as we relived our childhood under the care and love of Rosa and Sam Nobes in their little cottage nestling in the beauty of Bismore's 'Golden Valley'.

We sat talking at night, every night of my short stay. We joked and laughed and cried together as each spark of memory ignited a seemingly endless chain of recollection.

I recalled the day in Singapore in 1942 when a hundred of us, Australian prisoners, marched along Bukit Timah Road to our job of building a road through the jungle around a reservoir. It was a Sunday, the second Sunday in May. Suddenly, as we drew level with an avenue of low bushes, men darted from the ranks to snatch small sprigs

John and Flo.

of white blossom and fix them into their shirt pocket but-tonhole. Not to be left odd man out, I joined in the brief orgy, not really understanding the significance of the exercise. As I adjusted my spray to my pocket, I asked the chap next to me what it was all about.

'It's Mother's Day, Jack! You must never forget your mother.'

I was nineteen ... and I had just discovered my first Mother's Day.

'The real situation at that time,' I said, 'was that in reality I had two mothers.'

We sat pondering about this for some time and I studied her face. For an eighty-year-old she had worn pretty well. She still had the features I'd remembered and her abundant hair was a natural grey. But her pale brown eyes had retained much of their sparkle, although at this moment a distinct moist sadness reflected her sombre mood.

While this period of silence hovered around us, I decided that now was the time to share a secret I'd carried around for fifty-three years.

I spoke hesitantly, searching for suitable words and struggling to control my emotion at the memory of it all. I told Flo of the frightful event that took place on the last day of the battle for Singapore. It happened while our Company sat around eating a rare cooked meal beneath the shelter of a coconut plantation. A Japanese spotter plane approached our position but we paid little attention to its arrival. We had been observed before, but on this occasion we thought we were well hidden. However, no sooner had the plane passed over us, than we were caught in a relentless barrage of mortar bombs. It was too late to move, the bombing was too intense. We could only flatten ourselves on the ground. I had been sitting on the edge of a shallow drain so I flung myself into its slight protection. The bombing went on and on. There was no respite. It was terrifying. I put my hands over my ears to shut out the whooshing noise and explosion of each mortar bomb. The ground vibrated. I was sure I was going to die. And then it came. Something slammed into my back. It was hard earth but I didn't know it at the time. I just groaned. That was when I saw Mum's face. Rosa Nobes. 'I called out to her Flo. I couldn't stop myself. I cried out just one word ... Mother ...'